GETTING TO GRIPS WITH

Writing

CATHERINE HILTON
MARGARET HYDER

First published 1992

Editorial team
Rachel Grant, Andrew Thraves, Angela Royal

Design team
Frank Greenyer, Jonathan Barnard

Text © Catherine Hilton and Margaret Hyder 1992

© BPP (Letts Educational) Ltd
Aldine House, Aldine Place, 142-144 Uxbridge Road, London W12 8AW

British Library Cataloguing in Publication Data

Hilton, Catherine
    Writing. – (Getting to grips)
    I. Title II. Hyder, Margaret III. Series
    808.042

ISBN 1 85758 092 3

Printed and bound in Great Britain by BPCC Wheatons Ltd, Exeter

Acknowledgements

Page 30 'Jail mothers can keep their babies' by Frances Gibb ©Times Newspapers Ltd 1990; pages 33–4, from *On the House* by Simon Hoggart (Robson Books Ltd); pages 36–7, from *A Cruel Madness* by Colin Thubron (Reprinted by permission of William Heinemann Limited); page 38, from *The Ministry of Fear* by Graham Greene (William Heinemann Ltd, 1943); page 39, article reproduced by kind permission of *The Sun*; pages 40–41, 'Ring of Death' ©Times Newspapers Ltd 1990; pages 42–43, from an article in *Upbeat* magazine, published by Ringwood Publishing Ltd for BUPA; page 54, from *The Rain Forest* by Olivia Manning (William Heinemann Ltd); page 80, from *The Magic Apple Tree* by Susan Hill (Reproduced by permission of Hamish Hamilton Ltd); page 103, back cover of *The Fourth Protocol* by Frederick Forsyth (Corgi Books Ltd); page 108, from a promotional leaflet Champagne Flights International Ltd (Tel 0902 373293); page 110, from The Countryside Code (The Countryside Commission); page 177, from *The Seduction of Mrs Pendlebury* by Margaret Forster (Chatto and Windus); page 178, from *A Year in Provence* by Peter Mayle (Pan Books Ltd).

Contents

How to Use this Book 5

How to Use this Book

We hope that the advice and practice in this book will help you to

feel more confident about writing,

improve your writing skills,

gain more enjoyment from writing and

tackle a variety of writing tasks.

The book is divided into two sections.

SECTION 1 takes you through the various skills which make up the writing process.

▶ Constructing sentences

▶ Spelling

▶ Punctuating

▶ Writing in paragraphs

▶ Using a wide vocabulary

▶ Planning and organising ideas

It is advisable to work through the whole of Section 1 so that you can refresh your skills which will then give you the confidence to embark upon the various writing tasks in Section 2.

SECTION 2 opens with a chapter on summary skills as all the formal writing tasks within this section rely upon the use of proficient summary skills. Initially you will probably prefer to study those chapters which are most relevant to your needs. However, as you become a more accomplished writer we hope you will wish to extend your writing skills and will find the other chapters appropriate.

We have provided practice throughout the book as we feel that improving writing is an active process. Practice increases confidence; greater confidence helps you to gain more pleasure from writing.

1

Introducing Writing

There are times when writing appears to have been superseded by the telephone, tape recorder or video. While previous generations wrote letters to describe events, give information or convey feelings and ideas, today it is easy to pick up the telephone and speak to the other person directly. However, there are still occasions when we have to commit ourselves in writing.

everyday writing tasks	more formal writing tasks
	(These require higher standards of skill and accuracy.)
shopping lists	completing forms
notes to family and friends	formal or business letters
	memos
informal letters	essays for academic or vocational courses
	reports for work, clubs, societies, etc
	minutes; agendas

When you are required to write you may, like many people, regard writing as a chore: something that is difficult, which you delay starting or try to avoid. By developing your writing skills and your confidence you will find writing becomes not only more pleasurable and satisfying but also more effective.

What is effective writing?

We write for a number of different audiences and reasons but our aim is always the same: we are trying to communicate our ideas, thoughts, feelings or put our message across. This is the most important aspect of writing. If we wish to judge our writing, we must always look first to see whether we have communicated effectively before we consider other aspects.

Writing requires greater precision and care than speech as it is a more formal activity producing a permanent record. When we speak we can gauge our listener's response and clarify any points which haven't been comprehended. As no such interaction takes place in a piece of writing, our communication skills have to be unambiguous. Our writing will be effective if it is:

clear	It expresses our ideas carefully in a way that the reader can understand.
concise	It uses sufficient words to impart the message but not so many as to obscure the meaning.
exact	It uses vocabulary correctly and follows the conventions for spelling, punctuation and grammar.
appropriate	It uses the correct tone for the situation and the reader.

If you have doubts about the effectiveness of your writing, don't despair. It is possible to improve with guidance and practice.

▶ Actively consider the skills used in writing
▶ Develop your confidence
▶ Use the right tools

The writing skills

You have already seen that in order to write clearly, concisely, exactly and appropriately, certain skills and knowledge are needed.

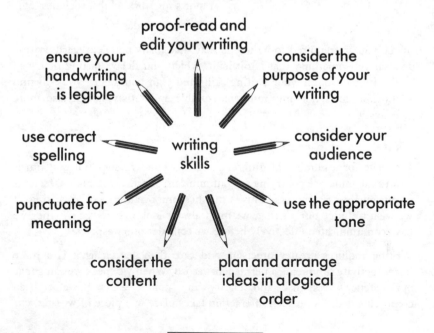

Purpose

Before you start a piece of writing, ask yourself two questions:

Why am I writing?

What do I want my writing to achieve?

Consider these questions before you think about the other aspects of writing.

You may be writing in reply to a letter, preparing a report at work, drafting an essay – **the reasons for writing are endless but the purpose must be clear in your own mind before you start.** (In Section 2 of this book you will be given guidance on writing for different situations and advised on the appropriate language, tone, style and layout.)

By thinking first about your purpose, you will find it easier to decide what you want your writing to achieve. For example, if you were writing to complain about a product, would you want the product repaired, exchanged or the price refunded? Determine your preference and then make sure you convey your wishes clearly.

Audience

Your aim in any piece of writing is that your reader, or audience, should understand and respond to your message. Your message must be expressed in the most effective way for that audience.

Who is your audience?

Do you know them?

What will they expect from you?

What might they be influenced by?

Most of us adopt a different style and language for different situations. When we talk to friends, we use the language and tone of voice appropriate to our relationship. In a formal situation we use more formal language, exact vocabulary and perhaps a more polite manner: **we should consider our audience and respond accordingly.** Our writing must also reflect this consideration.

Tone

Having considered purpose and audience, you will find the tone you need to adopt in your writing becomes clear. For example, a letter of complaint will have a formal, precise tone – firm but polite; a letter to a friend will be expressed in less formal language – a warmer and more relaxed tone will be evident.

The tone of a piece of writing is conveyed by the vocabulary, style, sentence structure and format of the writing. In later chapters you will be shown how you can create the correct tone by using the appropriate language and structures.

Planning

In any formal writing task it is essential to plan carefully before writing the first draft. The plan allows you to:

consider the content;

arrange your ideas in the most logical and acceptable order.

Careful planning will increase your chances of conveying your message effectively. In Chapter 7 you will be shown various ways of organising a plan and given guidance on how to assemble your ideas before writing.

Content

Considerations about content will vary according to the writing task and in Section 2 we will be looking at the content requirements of different types of activities in greater detail.

There are, however, some points regarding the content of a piece of writing that should *always* be considered.

Is the content relevant to the task?

Does your writing contain sufficient information or evidence for you to achieve your desired outcome?

Is it sufficiently interesting to engage your reader's atttention?

Remember, if the content is not suitable or adequate, your writing won't achieve its purpose.

Punctuation

Correct punctuation allows your reader to make sense of your ideas. A piece of writing which has no punctuation or is punctuated incorrectly is difficult or even impossible to understand and can convey the wrong message.

EXAMPLE:

> Last week we went to. Merry Hill Shopping Centre while Ann. And I shopped our two children. Were able to play in the. Children's playroom it made shopping a. Pleasure rather than a chore.

This passage is almost impossible to understand as the full stops have been put in the wrong places.

Expressing ideas in clear, correct sentences is an important writing skill. Correct sentence construction and punctuation will help you to impart your message effectively. If you haven't had the opportunity to do much formal writing for a few years, you may find that you need to brush up on your sentence construction and punctuation skills. Chapters 2 and 4 will help you with these aspects of writing.

Spelling

Many people feel inhibited about writing or say they can't write because they have difficulties with spelling. If you also feel that a lack of confidence about your spelling is stopping you from writing, it is important to put spelling into perspective. The degree of accuracy required depends upon the formality of the situation. For example, a diary entry written for your own pleasure or use may contain spelling errors, but a report written at work must be correctly spelt.

If accuracy is essential,

careful proof-reading of a first draft can eliminate obvious spelling mistakes;

knowledge of possible and probable spelling patterns will help you to identify problematical words;

sensible use of a dictionary will increase your confidence in your spelling.

Fear of making spelling mistakes should not stop you from writing. Chapter 5 looks at spelling in more detail and gives guidance on spelling patterns and techniques which we hope will make you feel more confident about the writing process.

Handwriting

Unless you are otherwise directed, you should use a cursive script when writing.

Use

cursive script

not

print

nor

CAPITAL LETTERS

When printing or writing in capital letters, you are more likely to make spelling mistakes because pausing between each letter impedes the smooth flow of the word and the sequencing of the letters. The flowing writing action of a joined script helps you to produce a correct spelling pattern instinctively.

Proof-reading and editing

It is rare for anyone to produce a good piece of writing at the first attempt. Most of us need to produce a rough or first draft before a final copy. Indeed, knowing that a first attempt can be edited and improved is very reassuring.

For formal writing tasks you will need to organise your thoughts and devise a plan before you embark upon the first draft.

Beginnings often cause difficulty – don't sit looking at a blank sheet of paper waiting for a polished first sentence to spring to mind: start writing and get your ideas down on paper. You should find that once you have started, your writing becomes more fluent.

When you have completed the first draft, follow these steps.

Read it through.

Ask yourself
does it fit the purpose?
is it effective?
are all the necessary points included?
is the tone appropriate for the situation?

Rewrite any parts you are unhappy about.

Reread – check for spelling and punctuation.
Make necessary changes.

Write your fair copy.

Proof-reading and editing may seem tedious but they are good practices to adopt and as you become more skilful and confident, you will find your first drafts need less improvement.

Develop your confidence

It may seem that writing involves so many skills that it is a daunting task, but it is possible to develop the necessary skills and with this development comes an increase in confidence. When you have worked through this book you will know many basic elements of writing and will then be able to use the book as a reference source if you encounter a problem or an unfamiliar writing task.

As with all skills, you will improve your writing skills by frequent practice: writing a few paragraphs a day is the best way to exercise your skills. Daily practice may take the form of personal writing (e.g. a diary) but don't limit yourself to writing about the same topics every day. Try to give yourself different types of writing tasks so that you develop a variety of styles and employ a wide range of words. Section 2 of this book will provide you with practice and may inspire you to develop your own themes or situations. **Seeing your writing improve through sustained practice will increase your belief in yourself as an effective communicator.**

Having the right tools

It is always easier to undertake a task if you work in the right conditions with the best facilities and equipment. Writing is no exception.

You will find that having a quiet working area helps you to concentrate on your writing. Without interruptions to your train of thought, your writing will become more fluent.

Although you may not use a dictionary and thesaurus now when you write, in Chapters 5 and 6 you will be shown how a sensible use of these books will improve and enhance your writing. When you are proof-reading, you may find it useful to have spelling, grammar and punctuation books to help you solve any problems. Although spelling, punctuation and grammar are referred to in this book, there is more detailed advice in the other books in this *Getting to Grips* series.

As you have already seen, writing and speech differ. You will probably find that you can express your ideas more readily in speech than in writing. It might help if you record your ideas on a dictaphone or tape recorder before you start writing. This will provide a useful prompt as you write.

Work can be checked in a similar way. If a piece of writing is particularly important or you are having serious doubts about your sentence construction, it is a good idea to read the piece of writing aloud in order to check it. You may find it useful to make a tape recording of this reading. When you play the tape, you will be able to concentrate on listening and so be able to identify any mistakes.

Some people are more confident about their writing when they use a computer or word processor because they can create text on a screen, delete words and move text around before committing it to paper. Most word processors and computers have a spell check facility, which is a useful aid for spotting spelling mistakes and increases confidence in the writing process. The spell check facility does, however, have its limitations. It will only be able to deal with words that have been programmed into its memory so some correct words may be questioned. (For example, personal names and place names.) Some spell checkers only recognise American spellings. A spell-checker will not identify incorrect choice. For example, if you typed 'I can't here' the spell check would not query 'here' as it is spelt correctly, even though 'here' doesn't make sense in this context.

Having access to these tools will make writing easier for you and may be instrumental both in the development of your writing and the enjoyment you gain from the writing process.

Final thoughts

You can improve your writing even if you consider yourself to be a poor writer. It may be that you haven't written for some time and some of your writing skills have rusted or you may not have received sufficient practical guidance about ways of improving. By working systematically through the relevant chapters in this book, following the advice given and adopting a careful attitude towards your writing, it will improve.

Before turning to the next chapter, pause and think about your writing.

Why do you want to improve your writing?

What opportunities for writing do you have?

Which aspects of writing do you find difficult?

How much time do you intend to set aside for practising?

How can you increase your writing opportunities?

2
Units of Sense – Sentences

Whenever we speak or write we do so because we have something to say and we want our message to be understood by our audience. In order for our message to be exact, clear and unambiguous it must be divided into units of sense. **Sentences are the natural units of speech and writing.**

> <u>Viking</u> South-west five or six. Showers. Moderate or good.
>
> <u>Biscay</u> Variable three. Rain then showers. Good.
>
> <u>Bailey</u> West veering north-west four or five. Showers. Good.
>
> <u>Wight Portland</u> Southerly. Rain later. Good becoming moderate.

Unless you know the code, you cannot decipher the information above as it isn't presented in units of sense. To gain meaning from these pieces of information, you need to be familiar with the format of the shipping forecast and understand what each piece of information refers to. If you knew that, in each case, the first piece of information after the sea area refers to the wind direction and speed, the second to the precipitation and the third to the visibility, you could make sense of the message. However, if the forecaster arranged this information in units of sense you wouldn't need to be familiar with the subject or its presentation.

> In the Viking area there will be south-westerly winds of force five or six. Although there will be some showers, the visibility will be either moderate or good.

Speaking

When we speak we usually arrange our speech into units of sense without being aware we are doing so.

GAVIN	When I phoned on Friday, I was told to come to the accommodation office today so that my accommodation could be sorted out.
DAVID	What is your name?
GAVIN	I'm Gavin Lambeth.
DAVID	Your form's here. You'll be in the hall opposite – number 118. Please can you complete these forms before you collect your key from the warden.

There are, however, times when you don't need to speak in sentences. Gestures, facial expressions and your audience's familiarity with the subject mean you can abbreviate your speech.

GORDON	Any luck?
REG	Four so far.
GORDON	Ripe?
REG	Over the top. Ugh!
GORDON	Here!

Writing

It is even more important to divide your message into units of sense when you write as you cannot use gestures, facial expressions or give your audience additional clues. Words are your only means of communication.

Often people say that they are concerned about writing because they cannot spell very well, but poor spelling, although it may let us down, doesn't usually prevent us from getting the message across to the reader. Failure to write in sentences can obstruct communication; sentences are the foundation of all writing.

Consider these three examples.

I do hope you will be able to attend the meeting on Monday September 6th is the beginning of the next course and we need to discuss our plans in advance all schemes should be submitted to me before the meeting

no punctuation

I do hope you will be able to atend the meating on Munday. Setembre 6th is the bigining of the nex corse and we need to disscus are plans in avanse. All skeems should be submitid to me befor the meating.

spelling errors

I do hope you will be able to attend. The meeting on Monday
September 6th is the beginning of the next course. And we
need to discuss our plans. In advance all schemes should be
submitted. To me before the meeting.

punctuation errors

As you can see, it is essential to write in sentences if your audience is to
understand your message.

Examiners frequently complain about candidates' failure to write in
sentences. Good content can be ruined by the misuse or omission of full
stops. Candidates often link a series of sentences together with commas
instead of dividing them into separate sentences.

In this chapter we will consider what a sentence is and look at some
different sentence structures. By understanding what constitutes a sentence
and recognising different sentence structures, it will help you to use a
variety of sentences in your writing.

What is a sentence?

> **sentence n.** a number of words making a complete grammatical
> structure, generally begun with a capital letter and ended with
> a full stop or its equivalent.

Every sentence must have:

> a **subject,**
> a **finite verb,**
> **and** make complete sense.

Sentences can be:

> **statements,**
> **commands** or
> **questions.**

A sentence begins with a capital letter and ends with a full stop, exclamation
mark or question mark.

The subject
In each sentence below, the subjects are in **bold print**.

1 **Brookfield Children's Farm** is on the southern outskirts of Balgowan.

2 **The report** was sent to the chairman.

3 **Freda** will collect her new car on Tuesday.

4 **The headmistress and her staff** welcomed the royal visitor.

5 **Books, clothing, compact discs and records** had all been strewn on the floor.

6 **It** was in the cabinet next to the model veteran car.

Every sentence must have a subject (or implied subject – see the section **Commands** later in this chapter).

The subject can be a single person or thing (as in sentences 1, 2, 3 and 6) or a group of people or things (as in sentences 4 and 5).

The subject of a sentence is usually a noun (or nouns) or a pronoun. (A noun is a 'naming' word; a pronoun replaces a noun.)

The subject is who or what the sentence is about.

Finite verb

Every sentence must have a finite verb. A finite verb is a verb which has a subject.

▶ A verb is a word of action,

EXAMPLES:

run

walk

think

ask

▶ or state of being.

EXAMPLES:

am

are

is

was

were

Some verbs are harder to identify than others. When a clear action is taking place, the verb is obvious. Verbs which express a state of being can be more difficult to identify.

A verb can consist of one word,

e.g. I **enjoy** Chinese food.

or need more than one word to express the tense.

EXAMPLES:

Sally **will be going** to Wales next weekend.

Naomi **has failed** her final exams.

The tense of the verb shows the time the action takes place, whether present, past or future.

EXAMPLES:

Sid is writing a letter. (present tense)

His son sits at the table. (present tense)

They answered the questions in record time. (past tense)

Mollie has retired because of ill health. (past tense)

I will collect my prescription tomorrow. (future tense)

My son is going to London later today. (future tense)

** Go back to the examples given under the heading **The subject** and identify the verb in each sentence.

Complete sense

Throughout this chapter we have stressed that a sentence is a unit of sense and that sentences are the cornerstone of clear writing.

A good way to test if what you have written is a sentence is to think of yourself standing on a busy main–line railway station. A stranger rushes up to you and says, "My cat had kittens yesterday." He then hurries away and is lost in the crowd. You may well be surprised by his behaviour but you can understand his message. If he had approached you and said, "Wearing a black mac," before disappearing into the crowd, you would have been more astonished. Who was wearing a black mac? Why hadn't he completed his message?

** Identify which of the following are not sentences. Remember, each sentence should have a subject, a finite verb and make complete sense.

1 Referring to your letter delivered last Saturday

2 Ian has been promoted

3 The school opening its gates to the public

4 At the side of the swimming pool

5 When the aircraft approached the runway

6 Last Tuesday all three children

7 After he had washed up

8 Suicide is illegal

9 Margery, anxious to be first

10 Approaching the bend in top gear

When you are engrossed in writing, it's easy to forget about complete sentences and end up with passages like this.

> As soon as she entered the room, she knew a burglary had taken place. The window open. The warm breeze in the room. Piles of books. Untidy heaps of clothes everywhere. Drawers half open Chaos.

** Rewrite the passage above in sentences. At the end, check each of your sentences and ask yourself if it makes complete sense. Check there is a verb and its subject in each sentence.

Statements, commands, questions

Sentences can be:

> statements,
>
> commands,
>
> or questions.

Statements

▶ Most of the sentences we speak or write are statements which express a fact or give an opinion.

EXAMPLES:

I don't think she has sufficient experience. (opinion)

The group discussed the possibility of using volunteers. (fact)

Councillor Newton outlined plans for helping disabled drivers. (fact)

I think Lake Thun is the most attractive lake in Switzerland. (opinion)

Water is represented by the chemical symbol H_2O. (fact)

Commands

EXAMPLES:

All of you leave the room immediately.

Clear the table.

Help me!

Albert, go away!

▶ A command, like a statement, must make complete sense.

▶ It can end in a full stop or an exclamation mark. An exclamation mark is used if the speaker delivers the command with emotion.

▶ The subject of each command is printed in colour. The second and third examples appear to have no subjects. The subject in each case is implied.

▶ The subject is also often omitted in sentences which offer advice or make requests.

EXAMPLES:

Please leave it for me to look at. (request)

Remember to proof-read your work. (advice)

In both examples the subject you is implied.

Questions

▶ A question is a special type of sentence. It ends in a question mark and a reply is expected.

EXAMPLES:

Are you ready?

Where's my dinner?

How many books did you buy?

Where do I collect my bag?

▶ The subject of each question is in coloured print. Each question has a finite verb and makes complete sense.

▶ A rhetorical question is a question to which no answer is either expected or required. It is frequently used by people addressing a large audience.

> I am here today to increase your awareness of Health and Safety in your own workplace. Are you aware of your responsibilities? Are there practices in your company which you turn a blind eye to? Are some Health and Safety considerations too costly to implement? We shall be considering these questions and many more during the course of the day.

The speaker is posing questions which he doesn't expect his audience to answer. Indeed, he would probably be upset if anyone interrupted his speech to answer his questions. Rhetorical questions still need question marks.

Applying the test

When you have completed any writing task, examine each sentence to make certain it can stand on its own and is a complete unit of sense.

Check

Is there a subject?

Is there a finite verb?

Does it make complete sense?

If you are uncertain, read each sentence aloud, pausing at the full stop so that you can ensure it makes sense before you read the next sentence. (Try the 'stranger on the station' test too.)

Types of sentences

A sentence can be any length. Read this passage and notice the varying lengths of the sentences and how they are constructed.

> In order that all part-time staff may be paid at the appropriate time, would they please submit a manual claim for the period up to and including Friday April 4th. Part-time staff who have already received a contract need not complete a manual claim as the computer will automatically generate their claims in the normal way.
>
> I am sorry that it has been necessary to revive the manual process on this occasion. All contracts will be issued by the next pay period.

Sentences can be classified as:

   simple,

   double,

   multiple

   or complex.

Simple sentences

A **simple sentence** has — a subject

                          a finite verb

EXAMPLES:

She <u>hung out</u> the washing.

It <u>rained</u>.

The plane <u>circled</u> overhead.

Bruno <u>barked</u>.

The angry shop keeper <u>served</u> the impatient customer.

Simple sentences can vary in length. Sentences are considered simple if there is only one finite verb.

People frequently make mistakes by joining two simple sentences with a comma.

e.g. The train was late, she missed it.

It is possible to join two or more simple sentences together as you will see later under double and multiple sentences, but they can never be joined by commas like this.

Double sentences

A double sentence consists of two simple sentences joined by a conjunction. It has two finite verbs.

EXAMPLES:

Brian **opened** the book but he did not **read** it.

The librarian **picked up** the disc and **placed** it in the computer.

These double sentences consist of two statements or main clauses linked by a conjunction ('but' in the first sentence; 'and' in the second). Both main clauses in each example are capable of standing alone.

When two main clauses are joined in this way, the subject of the second finite verb is often omitted.

EXAMPLES:

Brian opened the book but he did not read it.

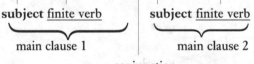

subject finite verb | **subject** finite verb

main clause 1 | main clause 2

conjunction

The librarian picked up the disc and placed it in the computer.

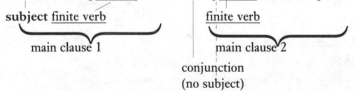

subject finite verb | finite verb

main clause 1 | main clause 2

conjunction
(no subject)

Sentences which don't have the same subject can also be linked together.

e.g. The train was cancelled. We caught the bus.

The train was cancelled but we caught the bus.

Use double sentences to achieve greater fluency; a series of simple sentences can produce a jerky writing style.

Multiple sentences

A multiple sentence may have three or more main clauses joined together to form one complete sentence.

EXAMPLES:

It rained and the wind howled but the match continued.

main clause 1   main clause 2   main clause 3

   conjunction   conjunction

She collected her pension and she walked to the bus stop and she sat under the shelter and she waited for the bus.

Each of the four main clauses has been underlined. Although it is technically possible to join four simple sentences in this way, the result is clumsy. The sentence could be improved by not repeating the subject (she) and removing two conjunctions.

She collected her pension, walked to the bus stop, sat under the shelter and waited for the bus.

Double and multiple sentences allow you to vary the length of the sentences you use, giving more variety and interest to your writing.

Complex sentences

A complex sentence can contain one or several main clauses and will have at least one subordinate clause.

A **main clause** is a clause which can stand alone.

A **subordinate clause** cannot stand alone and depends upon the main clause for meaning.

EXAMPLES:

When he was a student, he worked abroad every summer.

The man, whose car had been stolen on two previous occasions, decided to fit an alarm.

If I am to be successful, I must start applying for jobs now.

Knowing he was unable to win the race against such formidable odds, he feigned illness.

In each example the main clause has been underlined. Check that this main clause makes sense and can stand alone. The rest of the sentence is the subordinate clause. You will also see that the subordinate clause doesn't make sense on its own, but *depends* on the main clause for meaning. Hence a subordinate clause is sometimes referred to as a **dependent clause**.

e.g. My neighbour, who used to work in Hull, has a motorbike because she now works in Beverley.

The above sentence has two subordinate or dependent clauses.

Main clause: My neighbour has a motorbike

Subordinate clause 1: who used to work in Hull

Subordinate clause 2: because she now works in Beverley

Look at the words which introduce the subordinate clauses in the examples above and on the previous page.

when

whose

if

knowing

who

because

Other words which can be used at the beginning of a subordinate clause are listed below.

where	although	unless
which	before	while
that	though	whether
so	after	how
so that	as	why
until	as if	since

Such words form a link between the subordinate clause and the main clause even when they occur at the beginning of a complex sentence.

e.g. **Although** I have only just moved to the area, I am involved in many activities.

    link word

** Add a suitable subordinate clause to each of the following main clauses to form a complex sentence.

e.g. I fetched the newspaper

I fetched the newspaper when I went to the local shops.

1 Claud started to write an essay. . . .

2 We visited the needle museum. . . .

3 My aunt is almost 80. . . .

4 She helped herself to a slice of cake. . . .

5 He arrived home from work early. . . .

6 Our dog had an accident on Friday. . . .

** Combine each of the following groups of facts into one sentence. You may need to make minor alterations to the statements and you do not have to use the facts in the order they are presented.

1 The woman had blond hair. It had been carelessly arranged in a plait. She entered the shop. There was a long queue. She waited patiently to be served.

2 He adjusted his glasses. He blew his nose vigorously. He waited for the previous speaker to finish.

3 The doctor was tired. It was the end of a long day. He had his last patient to see. He called her into his consulting room.

4 Tim collected Angus. He drove them to Reeves Park. The Rock Festival was being held there. It was the town's first Rock Festival.

5 He had to catch the coach. It went from Alvechurch to Birmingham. The railway track was being electrified. No trains ran between 10 am and 5 pm.

6 Abdul lent his jacket to Andy. The jacket was made of leather. Andy could not go home to change. He had forgotten his keys.

7 Alison spread out her papers. She poured herself some water. She fingered her necklace nervously. She smoothed her skirt. She took a deep breath. Then she addressed the meeting.

8 He stood on the corner. He listened to the sound of the heavy artillery. It came from the hills. The hills were south of the town.

Good writing

Good writing should contain a variety of sentence lengths and structures. Be aware of this when you proof-read your writing.

▶ Too many short, simple sentences make your writing jerky and boring. Try to combine sentences to achieve greater fluency.

▶ Too many long sentences can confuse the reader, causing him to forget the subject of the sentence.

▶ Consider your <u>audience</u>,

the <u>pur<u>pose</u></u> of your writing,

and the <u>tone</u> you wish to adopt.

> Dear Sally,
>
> Last week I started my six weeks of compulsory work experience - there are five such periods in my three year course - with a firm of football pitch maintenance contractors which is situated in Solihull close to the M42 and five miles from my lodgings.
>
> To comply with the specifications, pitches have to be cut with appropriate machines which are fitted with tyres specifically designed to use on turf in order to produce a standard of finish in keeping with the particular use of the area; mounted gang mowers are used whenever possible....

Sentence lengths and structures should be appropriate to your audience, purpose and tone. For example, in this letter to a friend, the long, complicated sentences and formal language combine to give it a rather pompous tone which may bore the reader.

Different sentence lengths create different effects: a series of short sentences can create an atmosphere of excitement in a description or story.

Longer sentences are often needed when you want to present an argument, explain a process or give a detailed description: a short sentence placed after a series of longer sentences can create a dramatic effect.

Final thoughts

This chapter has looked at sentences in some detail as they are so important. **The sentence is the basic unit of writing, the hallmark of correct English. If you can write in clear sentences, your work will be understood.**

Knowledge of sentence construction will help you to punctuate sentences correctly, as you will see in Chapter 4.

3
Units of Sense – Paragraphs

In the previous chapter we concentrated on the importance of writing in natural units of sense: **sentences**. Here we will consider combining these individual units of sense into larger units: **paragraphs**.

Jail mothers can keep their babies

By FRANCES GIBB, LEGAL AFFAIRS CORRESPONDENT

THE Home Office appears to have backed down over removing babies aged nine months or more from mothers serving sentences prior to deportation. It is to investigate extending facilities at a closed women's prison so that mothers can have the older babies with them.

Last week, the National Association for the Care and Resettlement of Offenders, the Howard League and others protested about the enforced removal of older babies. The first such separation, expected last week at Holloway, north London, has not occurred.

Angela Rumbold, the Home Office minister, issued a statement saying that she was "very concerned" about two mothers at Holloway who were expected to be affected by the new policy and that she had taken steps to ensure that they would stay with their children.

She indicated a change in policy by the Home Office by saying that in the past babies could be held in closed conditions only until the age of nine months and adding: "There is a clear need that women who are subject to deportation and who, therefore, are not normally considered suitable for open conditions should be able to have their babies with them."

If you look at any piece of formal writing such as the extract from a newspaper opposite and the letter shown below, you will immediately notice, even without reading the passages, their visual arrangement into sections or paragraphs.

THE TENTING CLUB

PRESIDENT: R. CHAPMAN
CHAIRMAN: S. MAYO
DIRECTOR GENERAL: R. STEPHENS

MAYFLY HOUSE
BEVERLY WALK, NORTH ACTON HW2 4JZ
TELEPHONE: 04472 97240
TELEX: 55107   FAX: 04472 207692

September 1992

Dear Mr *Cooke*

We are pleased to enclose your new Membership card. The 12 months Club subscription is £19.00 plus £2.00 for each family member card required. Payment due will be debited from your account automatically, as authorised.

Should you wish to register with a Centre (see overleaf) please record your choice of Centre on the tear off portion of this letter and return it, using the envelope provided. Please do not fold the Centre Registration Advice. We regret that the Membership Department is not geared to handle any other enclosures. Such additional enclosures may be subject to delay in receiving attention.

If you do not wish to renew your membership, please notify the Membership Department before the subscription becomes due, and return the attached card.

Yours sincerely,

Ray Stevens

Director General

Why do we use paragraphs?

▶ A paragraph is a form of punctuation.

▶ Paragraphing helps our audience to make sense of our writing.

▶ Paragraphs act as signposts telling readers that a new idea or aspect is being developed.

▶ Good paragraphing makes it easier for readers to follow the stages of a piece of writing.

▶ Paragraphs give order and structure to our writing.

▶ If writing were not divided into paragraphs, it would be difficult and often daunting to read.

What is a paragraph?

paragraph: a collection of sentences having unity of purpose

People often complain that it is difficult to divide their writing into paragraphs because there are no clear guidelines which define what a paragraph really is. Such criticism is understandable as paragraphs do not begin at regular intervals and are not all of similar length; paragraphs start when they need to and go on for as long as necessary.

▶ A paragraph consists of a sentence or a series of sentences which forms a section of a complete piece of writing.

▶ An individual paragraph deals with one aspect of the subject you are writing about.

▶ A paragraph can be any length: begin a new paragraph when you have said all you want to about one idea or aspect and are ready to move on to the next.

▶ Each paragraph should have a central idea or theme.

▶ A paragraph usually has a key sentence.

Key sentences

The central idea or theme of a paragraph is often expressed in the first sentence or in a sentence near the beginning of the paragraph. The rest of the sentences in the paragraph will then explain, enlarge or illustrate this key sentence. A paragraph arranged in this way will have structure and unity and will be easy for the reader to follow.

In the following extract, each key sentence has been underlined.

The local council has erected a museum on one of the former
German bases. With the help of original film, documents,
maps, scale models and momentos donated by some of the
soldiers who took part in the landings, an interesting record
and fitting tribute has been created.

A few miles inland is the delightful small town of Sainte-
Marie-du-Mont. In this flat countryside, its domed
Renaissance church tower is visible from all directions. We
explored the town, following the plaques dotted around – each
relates an interesting anecdote about the liberation.

The wet, windy weather drove us south; we would explore
the landing beaches another year. We felt sure there would be
blue skies in the Loire Valley. The first part of our route,
along the N13, follows the 'Voie de la Liberté' – the route
taken by the liberators in 1944 – and there are frequent
markers along the roadside.

The site, Camping de Chatillon, is at the edge of the small
village of Huisseau sur Cosson which is about ten kilometres
south of Blois on the D33. It is an excellent camp site: clean,
well cared for, quiet and conveniently situated for numerous
chateaux. It is about four miles from the Chateau at Chambord
and it is possible to walk there through the vineyards across
the footpaths from the site.

Chambord, the largest of all the chateaux, was built by King
Francois I at the beginning of the 16th century. It was
continued by his son Henri II and finished by Louis XIV who
also had the park landscaped. It is fascinating to visit but allow
plenty of time as there are reputed to be 444 rooms.

**A paragraph is a group of sentences which relates to a theme. This
theme is often announced in the first sentence of the paragraph; the
rest of the sentences are arranged in a logical order to develop the
theme.**

** Read through the following passage several times. Identify the main ideas
then divide the article into paragraphs.

The House of Commons changes during the recess. Like a
stage when the curtains are drawn and the props dismantled,
large parts of it simply disappear. Seemingly half the

floorboards are raised, turning the corridors of power into hazardous catwalks, as scores of workmen lay wide, impressive-looking pipes. These are something to do with the new air-conditioning system. While the United States, which actually has hot weather, is learning to live without frozen air, the House of Commons, which is always in recess for two of the three summer months, is having it piped regardless of oil crises and Arabs. Huge quantities of furniture are moved from one place to another. Massive brown Chesterfields, displaced from the Smoking Room, line the Ways and Means corridor like slumbering hippos. Whole staircases are blocked off by multi-tiered piles of chairs. Vast rolls of carpet lie in wait to trip the hurrying visitor. In the Members' Lobby, now sealed off from an inquisitive public by arches of polythene sheeting, they are working on two stone plinths which stand on either side of the exit towards the Central Lobby. On one, it is said, Clement Attlee will shortly be raised. He will join Churchill, Balfour, Joe Chamberlain and other petrified politicians gazing out on the scurrying and scheming which whirls around the lobby when the house is sitting. The other plinth seems to be unaccounted for. One suggestion is that it should be devoted to the Unknown Lobby Correspondent. The sculptor would capture a facial expression devoted to world-weary cynicism and servility in equal measure, a pile of scruffy papers would be in his hand, and at his feet would stand the Eternal Gin and Tonic. In the midst of the works, by the Commons rifle range, there was last week a large colourful notice headed THINK METRIC. Underneath was a drawing of a large foot, and the legend: "This is not a foot. It is 300 millimetres." Someone had scrawled underneath: "And who is going to 300 millimetre the bill for all this load of trash, then?"

(from *On the House* by Simon Hoggart)

Planning your writing

In Chapter 1 you were advised to plan your writing and in Chapter 7 you will be given more detailed advice about gathering ideas and planning. You will often find that each aspect of your plan can form a paragraph.

EXAMPLE:

You need to write a letter to a customer who has complained about a product. You make a list of all the points you need to include.

1 thank for letter – date received

2 sympathise with problem, understand their point of view

3 outline your position

4 sorry can't help

5 future advice for customers

The points in your list are already arranged in logical order and each will form a paragraph.

If a piece of writing has been properly planned, paragraphs will tend to be quite obvious. Every time a new subject is introduced or a new development of the theme takes place, a new paragraph will be needed.

If you plan your work, paragraphs should develop quite naturally.

Forming paragraphs

Thinking about the structure of each paragraph should also be part of the planning process.

▶ When you have identified an idea or theme which you wish to develop as part of your piece of writing, **think of a clear key sentence** which will introduce this idea or theme to your audience.

▶ The rest of the sentences in the paragraph should then be **arranged in a logical order** to help steer your reader through the paragraph.

▶ When you have said all you want to say about this idea or theme, **move on to the next idea and begin a new paragraph.**

▶ **Don't keep changing tense** either within a paragraph or from one paragraph to another. More advice about tense will be given in Chapter 12. It is generally easier to write in the past tense. Although the present can make writing vivid and immediate, it is often difficult to sustain.

▶ **Don't stray from one topic to another** within a paragraph.

▶ Try to begin your paragraphs in a variety of ways.

▶ It is usual to indent each paragraph to make the new paragraph obvious to the reader. In business correspondence it is common to leave a line between paragraphs instead of indenting them.

▶ If you forget to indent a paragraph in an examination or a piece of coursework, you can use the symbol of two diagonal parallel lines (//).

▶ The first paragraph of any piece of writing is particularly important as it sets the scene or the tone. It should have the effect of making the reader want to read further. When you choose a book to buy or borrow, you may well read the first few paragraphs. If these do not hold your attention, you are unlikely to choose the book.

▶ The importance of the last paragraph should not be overlooked either. This can form the final impression that the reader may carry away with him.

▶ Try to form a **natural link** between one paragraph and another. You can often develop a thread from the previous paragraph to introduce the next.

** Read through the following passage and see if you can identify the links between the paragraphs.

I've been here half my life. I was here ten years ago, when I met Sophia. I arrived eleven years before that. And I still haven't gone.

It must be one of the most run-down preparatory schools in the country. Sunningrove: imagine a four-storey brick colossus louring above windswept playing-fields, an undersized swimming-pool and a few outbuildings set aside for inessentials (music, art). The school colours are red and green, which is grotesquely right. Brick, grass. There's little else in sight. The only expression on the colossal red face is a dribble of black fire-escapes, running from roof to earth like disastrous worry-lines. The playing-fields slope away to woods, which are out-of-bounds and where a lake is sunk in a bed of rhododendrons, which flower for two weeks at the start of the summer term, then return to darkness. The lake's gloom is exacerbated by memory: before my time one of the school cooks drowned herself in it. The whole surface is glazed by a pale green scum, broken here and there by concentric rings, where something might have dropped in years ago. All around, the rhododendrons' bodies are gouged out by the dens and passageways of the boys, and gape like caves wherever they have been entered. Nobody obeys the out-of-bounds rule. Only when McQuitty wants to punish a boy, and can't find a specific excuse, he'll say "*You were seen in the woods.*"

Three generations of McQuittys have run the place now. Their portraits adorn the dining-room much as the framed photographs of presidents watch over the offices of East

European states. Their expressions are subsumed by a common, prestigious deadness, as if the headmastership immunised them from human frailty. They don't smile. They look down from another stratosphere on the long tables with their watery porridge or wafer-thin beef (every other Saturday) and prunes or rice-pudding (Tuesdays) as though they had nothing to do with it. But their hypocrisy is plain, because beneath the portrait of the youngest incumbent, James R. McQuitty M.A., sits the living flesh. The painted man is grave, scholastic even; his unindented cheeks and little greenish eyes might be construed – if not as benign (the portrait-painter has his integrity), then at least as harmlessly abstracted. But underneath this symbol sits the actual McQuitty, unconscious of incongruity. He is formidably gross. The hair is greying from his head in a russet dust, and the jowls slop and shudder over his collar. Seen from behind, the red bulge of his neck is as broad as the head above it. But he is only forty-seven. He emanates a kind of predatory unease, restless with something I don't know. He isn't married (the grotesque dynasty will die with him). When he smiles his face's fatness hardens into little orbs and bulges of veined flesh, and his small, even teeth glint in warning. He is obsessed by the school's decline, because once – in the lifetime of the portraits hanging beside his – it had reputation. Their stares must be unbearable. The place has gone downhill in the insidious, half noticeable way that institutions do. A worse class of boy was attracting a worse type of teacher, he had told me when he hired me twenty years ago (Christ) and he meant to change all that.

But he never did. A fog of failure hangs over the staff – of failure not in their school duties, but in that they are here at all, in this cul-de-sac.

I, too. When I think that I came here to fill in time while deciding *what to do with my life*. In twenty years I've graduated to renting two rooms in the staff wing instead of one. I can play my Hi-Fi after ten o'clock without the assistant maths master banging on the wall with a shoe. Once McQuitty told me I was 'deputy-headmaster material'. I smiled back into those green eyes and felt my next twenty years, my whole life, being swallowed up. Then I went out and, literally, was sick down the lavatory.

(from *A Cruel Madness* by Colin Thubron)

Paragraph links

In this passage, the <u>first paragraph</u> ends with a reference to the reader still being 'here' (Sunningrove). This sets the scene for Sunningrove to be described in paragraph two.

The description in <u>paragraph two</u> ends with a reference to McQuitty. <u>Paragraph three</u> then describes the McQuitty family in general and James McQuitty in particular.

<u>Paragraph three</u> ends with McQuitty's intention to make changes and <u>paragraph four</u> begins with his failure to do so.

<u>Paragraph four</u> ends by referring to the lack of opportunities for the staff; <u>paragraph five</u> refers to the writer's own hopeless position.

If you are writing dialogue, remember to start a new paragraph for each speaker.

EXAMPLE:

"Then all we have to do is sit and wait. We might ring up the restaurant and order dinner. Lots of courses, and a good wine. Travers can pay. We'll begin with a very dry sherry."

"Yes," Miss Hilfe said, "if we were sure the right waiter would bring it."

He smiled. "You think of everything. It's the continental training. What's your advice?"

"Ring up the clerk – we know him by sight. Make trouble about something. Insist that he must come along, and then we'll walk out with him."

"You're right," he said. "Of course that's the way."

He lifted the curtain and she followed him. "What are you going to say?"

"I don't know. Leave it to the moment. I'll think of something." He took up the receiver and listened ... and listened. He said, "I think the line's dead." He waited for nearly two minutes, but there was only silence.

"We *are* besieged," she said. "I wonder what they mean to do." They neither of them noticed that they were holding hands: it was as though they had been overtaken by the dark and had to feel their way ... .

(from *The Ministry of Fear* by Graham Greene)

In good writing you should be able to identify the idea or theme in each paragraph and see that all the sentences within the paragraph support, expand, illustrate or supplement the central idea or theme.

Using paragraphs

The same can be said of paragraphs as of sentences: use a variety of lengths and structures within a piece of writing.

Too many short paragraphs can produce a jerky, disjointed effort whereas a profusion of long paragraphs may intimidate or confuse your reader.

The length of paragraphs depends on your

purpose,

audience,

and tone.

Short paragraphs

Examiners may disapprove of too many short paragraphs in an essay because these may indicate that the candidate is unable to develop his ideas.

Tabloid newspapers nearly always use short paragraphs, as the article below illustrates.

Villains on bail do 4 in 10 crimes

FOUR out of 10 crimes are committed by crooks let out on bail, police revealed yesterday.

A survey shows a wave of thefts by teenage villains freed by courts as soon as they are caught.

The Home Office is now being urged to stamp down on the 1976 Bail Act.

One youngster admitted carrying out 274 crimes while out on bail, said the Northumbria police report.

The survey, taken over a year, showed that of 12,247 crimes, 4,915 were committed by people on bail.

(from the *Sun* newspaper)

Short paragraphs enable the journalist to convey a number of facts or ideas in a small space. The intention is to give the reader a taste of the news and not an in-depth report.

A short paragraph placed among a series of longer paragraphs can be effective. It can provide contrast, a change of pace and produce a dramatic effect. It gains the reader's attention.

Long paragraphs

Text books often contain long paragraphs which may be necessary to convey detailed information. In your writing it is best to guard against overlong paragraphs as they can confuse your reader and even you – the writer. It is easy to lose sight of the main theme of the paragraph as you write.

When you proof-read your writing, you may find that you have several long paragraphs. Check each paragraph to ensure that you have not strayed from one theme to another within the same paragraph.

Balanced paragraphs

In a piece of writing which examines, develops and weighs up various arguments you are more likely to produce paragraphs of similar length as the article below illustrates.

RING OF DEATH

An element of danger exists in many sports. Horse racing, rock climbing, Formula One, even rugby, all carry a chance of death or severe disability comparable with that in boxing. But boxing is the only sport in which the aim is to cause injury. The boxer's intention is to disable his opponent's brain with a knockout. In boxing's brutality lies a central part of its appeal.

Since the Marquess of Queensbury's rules were introduced in 1884, in response to public disquiet at the horrors of bare knuckle prize fighting, some 500 boxers have died in the ring. Many more have been reduced to shambling wrecks, sweeping up in the gyms where they once trained.

Nonetheless, boxing has provided hope for countless young men who found in its discipline and skills a way of escape from poverty. A sport that had brutality as its sole appeal would never have inspired writers as diverse as Hemingway, Shaw, A. J. Liebling or Norman Mailer. Great fighters display a courage in the ring that wins them intense public affection. Frank Bruno and Henry Cooper provide examples of gentlemanly behaviour that few other sports can match. It is precisely because boxing is worth preserving that it needs urgent reform.

To be safer, championship fights ought to be shorter. An exhausted boxer in the later rounds is more vulnerable to a heavy blow than at the start. The safety record is much better in amateur bouts, which last only three rounds. Professional championship contests have been reduced from 15 rounds to 12, but most professional fights last at most eight or ten. That is enough.

Other safety measures should be closely examined. In Japan regular brain scans are compulsory. They should be here, too, both before and after fights. Heavier gloves and head protectors might reduce injury, although some doctors believe that it is the force of the blow that damages the brain and these will do little to reduce its impact. A longer break between rounds may help referees to judge better when a fighter must be told that he cannot go on. But reformers should beware of sanitising the sport to the point where it goes underground. Unlicensed boxing, and even illegal bare knuckle fights, appear to be growing, with potentially deadly consequences.

Boxing will never be entirely safe. But it must be made less unsafe. If the sport is to survive, boxing authorities here and in America must change the rules. If they continue to sit on their cornerstools, they should not be surprised if the politicians decide to abolish the ring.

(from *The Times*)

In such discursive writing you tend to give equal consideration to each argument you develop.

Summing it up

If you plan your paragraphs carefully you are less likely to produce too many short or too many long paragraphs.

In the planning process you may identify ideas which have little evidence to support them. You might then question whether they are really integral to your argument. You might also discover points which have too much supporting evidence. Perhaps it would be better either to omit some of this evidence or break down your ideas into a number of more manageable units, each forming the basis of a separate paragraph.

Final thoughts

▶ Most formal writing, whether in books, newspapers, letters, reports, essays or memoranda, is divided into paragraphs.

▶ If you want to produce well-written informal letters that your audience will readily understand, you should also use paragraphs.

▶ Writing without any paragraphs shows an examiner that you haven't planned your work. Your writing will lack structure.

▶ Plan your piece of writing and then plan each paragraph.

▶ Each paragraph should be concerned with one aspect, idea or theme.

▶ Make certain all the sentences within a paragraph are relevant to the theme.

▶ When reading good books, newspapers or magazines, look carefully at writers' paragraphing.

Ask yourself

Does it help the reader?

Can you see the main idea of each paragraph?

Do all the sentences in the paragraph support the main idea?

Are there too many short, jerky paragraphs?

Are there too many long, tedious paragraphs?

By being critical of the writing of others, you will become critical about your own writing.

** Read through this article several times and then apply the checklist above. List the main idea or theme of each paragraph. If you feel the paragraphs are either too short or long, alter the paragraphing.

EASTERN PROMISE

Open a Japanese lunch box and you might find a colourful display of raw fish, rice balls wrapped in seaweed, a tiny rolled omelette, pickles, crunchy raw vegetables and a fan of fruit pieces. Compare the British counterpart with its soggy sandwich, bag of crisps, bar of chocolate and fizzy drink and you begin to see the difference between us and the Japanese.

The Japanese care about food – not just its nutritional value but how it looks and how it tastes. In food lessons, Japanese schoolchildren are taught to eat 30 different foods a day and aim for 100 a week. Their lunchboxes reflect the philosophy that variety will provide the range of nutrients that the Japanese feel they need for health.

Even though they smoke and have a history of eating salty, pickled food (giving them the world's highest level of gastric cancer), the Japanese have the highest life expectancy in the world. They also have the lowest rate of heart disease (England's coronary death rate is six times as high) and their average cholesterol level is 30 per cent lower than ours. Interestingly, Japanese people who move out of Japan and adopt a Western lifestyle and diet acquire the same risk of heart disease as the rest of us.

So what are the benefits of the

Japanese diet? Donald Naismith is Professor of Nutrition at King's College Hospital, London: "The traditional Japanese diet is high in starch from rice, low in saturated fat and high in fish oils, which may have beneficial properties. They eat a lot of vegetables so have a good intake of vitamin C and beta carotene which protect against diseases such as cancers. They used to eat lots of salty, pickled food which is associated with strokes and stomach cancer. However, since more food is stored in the fridge these days, the consumption of this sort of food is now lower and the incidence of stomach cancer has decreased. Of course, lifestyles are changing and they are eating a lot more meat and Western food. They are even growing bigger. But they still live the longest."

(from *Upbeat* magazine)

4
Punctuation in Practice

We have already considered the importance of punctuation: in Chapter 1 where it was referred to as one of the essential writing skills, and in Chapter 2 which examined the basic units of all writing – sentences. In this chapter we will look at the punctuation which is needed within sentences themselves.

What is punctuation?

It is one of the writing skills.

It is an established code of signs which allows people to make sense of our reading and writing.

It separates one group of words from another.

Why is it important?

It allows others to understand our message.

It gives our readers clues and special information.

It makes our writing clear, exact and unambiguous.

- capital letters
- commas
- semicolons
- colons
- dashes
- apostrophes
- quotation marks

The intention of this chapter is to give a brief and basic guide to punctuation. If you feel you need more detailed advice, refer to the *Punctuation and Grammar* book in this *Getting to Grips* series.

If you write, you must punctuate.

Although there are certain basic rules which we will outline in this chapter, there are also personal preferences, but remember that **the main purpose of punctuation is to help our reader make sense of our writing**.

Chapter 2 looked at the punctuation marks which separate one sentence from another.

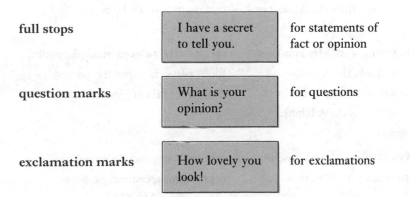

full stops   I have a secret to tell you.   for statements of fact or opinion

question marks   What is your opinion?   for questions

exclamation marks   How lovely you look!   for exclamations

If we always wrote in short sentences we would have little need for other punctuation marks but good writing should contain a variety of sentence lengths and structures which need additional punctuation marks to separate groups of words and give our reader extra clues.

Capital letters

Capital letters are used for specific purposes and give our readers useful clues.

Then Belinda R. Curtis smiled.

beginnings of sentences
people's names – first
names, surnames, initials

Ann replied, "My new address
is: Mantons, 3 Grove Street,
High Hinton, St. Austell,
Cornwall."

first word within speech marks
place names, e.g. house names,
roads, districts, counties

I am English but I live in France
and speak German at home.

the personal pronoun: 'I'
names of countries, nationalities
and languages

One Saturday in April I saw
Tim's photos of the Gobi
Desert and the Atlas Mountains.

days of week, months of year
specific places, e.g. named deserts,
mountains, rivers, lakes, oceans,
continents, etc.

On Boxing Day Mrs Hopkins
went to sees the Japanese
version of 'Jesus Christ
Superstar' at the Adelphi
Theatre.

special days, titles of musicals, books,
films, plays, newspapers, poems,
T.V. and radio programmes, etc.

My company, United Biscuits,
gave me a Ford Granada.

other proper nouns, e.g. makes of cars,
organisations, companies, brand
names, special buildings, etc.

Testing out capital letters

** Insert all the necessary capital letters in this passage.

> sarah newton had intended to stay at the hotel imperial in
> torquay for christmas, but when she saw the advertisement in
> pickfords travel for winter holidays in florida, she changed her
> mind. an american christmas appealed to her so she rushed
> into the shop. "have you any places left? i would like to go to
> florida next monday – that's christmas eve."

Commas

Commas can confuse people as there are instances when they are a matter of personal taste. However, there are situations when commas are always required.

A comma is used within a sentence to separate one group of words from another to clarify its meaning.

If you leave out a comma, it can confuse your reader.

"When he arrives go immediately." (confusing)

"When he arrives, go immediately." (clear)

Using a comma instead of a full stop to link two separate sentences together is a basic punctuation error.

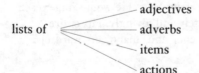

use commas
- in lists
- in dialogue
- in letters
- for asides
- to separate main clauses from subordinate clauses

Lists

Commas help the reader to sort one item from another and make sense of a list.

lists of
- adjectives
- adverbs
- items
- actions

Adjectives
EXAMPLES:

Her husband is <u>morose</u>, <u>unsociable</u> and <u>argumentative</u>.

She cradled the <u>large</u>, <u>blue</u>, <u>chipped</u> cup in her hands.

Adverbs

As the rope snapped, he fell <u>quickly</u>, <u>heavily</u> and <u>awkwardly</u>.

Items

During a term's woodwork he had completed <u>a cup stand</u>, <u>a bird box</u>, <u>a trinket box</u> and <u>a book shelf</u>.

Actions

Each morning Sally <u>made the beds</u>, <u>washed the dishes</u>, <u>prepared a picnic lunch</u> and <u>took her sons to school</u>.

Helpful Hints

▶ No comma is needed between the final adjective and the noun it describes.

▶ Usually there is no need for a comma before the conjunction which separates the last two 'units' of a list.

▶ In certain instances it is helpful if you place a comma before the final 'and' in a list of items.

e.g. He had a large collection of old records by 'Jerry and the Pacemakers', 'Cliff Richard and the Shadows', and 'Sonny and Cher'.

This comma helps to separate one group of performers from another; the reader may be confused without it.

** Insert all the necessary commas in this passage. (You will notice how difficult reading is when there are no commas to help you.)

Claud was enthusiastic about his collection of toy soldiers railway engines stamps and carrier bags. He spent every Saturday morning dusting the soldiers oiling the engines and cataloguing the stamps and carrier bags. He would finger each new treasure slowly deliberately and lovingly. His entire collection was housed in the enormous mahogany wardrobe next to his bed.

Dialogue

e.g.   'No, he's not here, Jim,' she called.

separates 'yes' or 'no' from the rest of the sentence in an answer	separates person's name when he is being addressed	separates the words enclosed in the speech marks from the rest of the sentence.

We don't have a great deal of opportunity to write and punctuate dialogue as it is generally only used in English essays, but it is worth appreciating how it is punctuated so that you have the freedom to include it in your essays if you wish to. More advice is given about punctuating dialogue later in this chapter.

Letters

greetings	salutations	addresses
Dear Ivy,	Yours sincerely,	4 Hunt Avenue,
	Yours faithfully,	Church End,
		Bideford,
		Devon.

If you type letters, then you probably omit this punctuation but in handwritten letters it is customary to include it. Further advice is given in Chapter 9.

Asides

EXAMPLES:

Fortunately, she had warned him yesterday.

I wonder, however, if it is necessary.

Her mother, whom I met for the first time last year, is still very attractive.

My sister, the youngest of five children, is about to emigrate.

Asides can consist of one word or a group of words. They give us additional information but they can be omitted; they are not crucial to the main thrust of the sentence and so are separated from it by commas.

To separate main and subordinate clauses

EXAMPLES:

If I leave now, I will catch my train.

subordinate clause   main clause

When the train finally pulled into the station, many of the commuters jumped off.

subordinate clause   main clause

A main clause is the main part of a sentence which makes its own statement and can stand alone.

A subordinate or dependent clause gives additional information about the main clause but cannot stand on its own.

Summing it up

Follow the guidelines for using commas but also use your common sense.

** Read these pairs of sentences and decide which sentence in each pair is the clearer of the two.

1 However I like Audrey.

However, I like Audrey.

2 Cliff entered the classroom with his wife and his books in a carrier bag.

Cliff entered the classroom with his wife, and his books in a carrier bag.

3 In particular trousers are forbidden.

In particular, trousers are forbidden.

4 With this in mind time will be available towards the end of the day.

With this in mind, time will be available towards the end of the day.

Helpful Hints

▶ Commas shouldn't interrupt the flow of sentences; they are only used to clarify meaning.

▶ Although it is the shortest of the punctuation pauses, the comma's position can greatly affect the meaning of a sentence.

▶ If you can use sentence enders (full stops, question marks, exclamation marks) and commas correctly, you should be able to write clearly and effectively and may not see the need to use semicolons, colons or dashes. However, these marks give you greater flexibility and provide variety in your writing.

Semicolons

These are used to:

> link two closely related sentences;

e.g. I will be away tomorrow; I will also be absent on Thursday.

> join sentences which show a strong contrast;

e.g. My son is very serious; my daughter is always laughing.

or separate items in a long or complicated list.

e.g. Bret's favourite rooms were: the Armoury on the ground floor; the Victorian kitchen, housed in the old chapel; the squire's office, still as the last occupant had left it in 1903; and the servants' quarters on the third floor.

As there are already commas within some of the items in the list, additional commas to separate each complete item may confuse the reader – semicolons are better.

Colons

You will probably be familiar with using a colon to introduce a list as in the sentence above beginning, "Bret's favourite rooms were: the Armoury ...".

A colon can also be used **to divide one part of a sentence from another where the second part expands, summarises or explains the first part.**

e.g. I had to leave: he threatened to kill me.

Dashes

A single dash can be used in a similar way to a colon. Used at the end of a sentence, **it can introduce an explanation or indicate a dramatic pause.**

e.g. The judge announced his verdict – innocent.

A pair of dashes acts like a pair of commas or brackets **to separate an aside.**

e.g. I found – as I rummaged through his bedroom – a clue to his disappearance.

Apostrophes

An apostrophe is used for:

contractions

and with nouns to show ownership.

Contractions

We frequently use contractions in conversation.

don't	for	do not	we'll	for	we will or we shall
I'm	for	I am	where's	for	where is

An apostrophe is used to replace the missing letters.

Always check that you have placed the apostrophe in the exact position of the missing letters.

Such contractions should only appear:

▶in informal writing

▶in dialogue as part of an essay

Ownership

Apostrophes often concern and confuse writers but they are not difficult to use if you follow the guidelines.

▶If there is one owner, place an apostrophe after the 'owner' and add 's'.

e.g. My aunt's <u>glasses</u> were next to my brother's <u>plate</u>.

In each case the word with the apostrophe is the owner; the underlined word is the owned item.

owner	owned
aunt	glasses
brother	plate

e.g. All the employees' lockers had been forced open by the thieves' crowbars.

owners	owned
employees	lockers
thieves	crowbars

▶In each case there is more than one owner – employees, thieves. An apostrophe has been added after the plural word for the owners.

Rules for using the apostrophe to show possession

▶If there is one owner,

write the owner's name,

place an apostrophe after it,

then add 's'

▶If there is more than one owner,

write the word for the owner,

place an apostrophe after it.

It is the word for the owner or owners which must have an apostrophe.

Special cases

These words each have an irregular plural form:

children   women   men

When they become owners, the apostrophe is placed after the plural word and an 's' is added.

children's opinions   women's choices   men's decisions

Is there an owner? ➡ No apostrophe is needed.

No

Yes

Is there one owner?
Is there more than one owner?

one owner

more than one owner

Write the word.
Add an apostrophe.
Add 's'.

Write the plural word.
Add an apostrophe.

Remember, for irregular plurals
add an apostrophe and an 's'.

4

Quotation marks

Speech

You will have already seen quotation marks in use for speech earlier in this chapter under the section on commas. Quotation marks enclose the actual words a person says.

EXAMPLES:

"The carrots need thinning out," grumbled Andrea.

"Shall I open it now?" Clive enquired.

"It's useless!" he stormed.

► A comma, question mark or exclamation mark separates the words within the quotation marks from the rest of the sentence. Such marks are placed inside the quotation marks.

► The first word within the quotation or speech marks begins with a capital letter.

e.g. "I won't," she fumed, "stay here to be insulted."

► However, when a sentence is interrupted by words like 'she fumed', the first word within the speech marks which follows the interruption begins with a lower case letter.

► In a passage of dialogue a new paragraph is needed to indicate the change of speaker. It helps the reader to follow the conversation.

EXAMPLE:

"That's a disgusting sight," she said.

Simpson flirtatiously asked: "What is, young lady?"

"That fish. What *point* in killing these harmless creatures? It's slaughter. Savagery. It's degrading."

Simpson, his brows and moustache a-twitch, could not speak at first, and then broke out brusquely: "What's it to do with you?"

"Everything. The creatures of the world belong to all of us. When you kill them, you rob everyone."

(from *The Rain Forest* by Olivia Manning)

Quotation marks can be written as double (" ") or single (' ') marks. The choice is yours but it is perhaps sensible to use double marks for speech and single marks for other purposes, such as quotations and titles of plays, books and films.

Quotations

When you want to quote a passage from a newspaper, magazine, book or any other source, you enclose the quotation within quotation marks to show your reader that these are not your own words but someone else's.

e.g. The author considers that, 'Of all the 26 miles of footpaths spreading out over the Malvern Hills, none is more popular than that which scales British Camp.'

You will notice that there is a comma before the quotation begins. You may use a colon instead of a comma if you wish.

Titles

When you write the title of a play, pantomime, book, film, radio or TV programme, poem, newspaper, magazine, etc., you should signpost this for the reader by including the title in quotation marks.

e.g. He said, "I enjoyed watching 'Jewel in the Crown' which was based on Paul Scott's novel, 'The Raj Quartet'."

Final thoughts

4

▶ Although you shouldn't worry unduly about punctuation, it is an essential writing skill – lack of punctuation, or faulty punctuation, can distort your message. If you want your readers to make sense of your writing, then you must provide them with adequate clues: the correct punctuation marks.

▶ Always proof-read your writing. Make a special check for punctuation.

Have you written in sentences?

Have you included the correct punctuation marks within each sentence?

▶ If you feel you understand the basics of punctuation, you will be able to write freely and confidently.

▶ Good punctuation comes with practice.

Write as frequently as you can.

Read well-written newspapers, magazines and books and notice how other writers use punctuation.

5
Spelling

Spelling is only one aspect of writing but it is the one that people most often blame for their writing difficulties. When writing, some people restrict themselves to using only the words they feel confident about; others believe that if they could spell they would be able to produce perfect writing.

As we have already stressed in Chapter 1, it is essential to consider spelling as just one of the writing skills. It is particularly important in formal writing, but:

> don't let spelling difficulties inhibit your writing;
>
> don't avoid writing – spelling is a skill and like all other skills goes rusty if it is not used.

It is possible to improve and develop more confidence in your spelling. This chapter will provide you with a basic framework which you can continue to build upon. As this chapter covers numerous spelling points, you may need to return to parts of it and use it as a reference source.

You can improve your spelling

| Confidence |
| Determination |
| A careful attitude |

Confidence

Confidence comes from knowing how to tackle a spelling problem. Use appropriate techniques to help you to learn and recall spellings.

▶ Write as often as possible – using not only the words you can spell but also tackling those you are less certain about.

▶ Believe you can improve, don't write yourself off as a poor speller.

▶ Recognise your improvement and acknowledge your success: confidence thrives on success.

Determination

determination

to learn   to use techniques   to practise

Learn

Select words to learn that are relevant to you. Identify your priority words – those that you use frequently or know would be useful. These words may be from your:

> personal life,
>
> work,
>
> academic or vocational studies, or
>
> social or leisure activities.

Select a few words to learn each week, find suitable techniques and keep practising. You may find it useful to list your priority words in a personal word book or create a special computer file.

Techniques

There are various techniques you can adopt to help you learn spellings. Different techniques suit different words and people find certain techniques more successful than others.

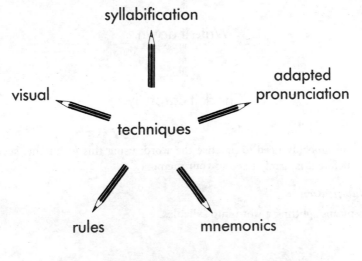

Visual technique

Spelling is primarily a visual skill. Good spellers can 'see' a word and transfer that image onto paper. They appear to be able to write effortlessly without having to consider spelling. If you have difficulty remembering words visually, concentrate your attention on the shape of words.

e.g.

Notice the length of the word, the 'l', 'p', 'g' and the letter pattern – all of which help to create this word's distinctive shape.

Words will only have distinctive shapes if they are written in lower case letters.

If you wish to learn a word by using the visual technique, follow this procedure.

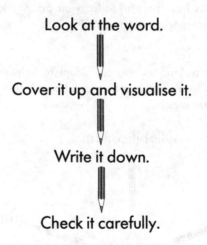

You will probably need to practise the word, using this technique, several times before it is firmly fixed in your memory.

Syllabification

This means splitting a word into syllables.

A **syllable** is a word or part of a word uttered by a single effort of breath.

Words may contain one, two or several syllables.

EXAMPLES:

peach (one syllable)

ear/ly (two syllables)

hap/pin/ess (three syllables)

pho/to/cop/i/er (five syllables)

There are rules for dividing words into syllables but it may be better to follow your own preference and split words in ways that are most helpful to you. It is a useful technique because it:

helps you to break long words into smaller, more manageable parts,

gives you the confidence to tackle long words,

stops you leaving out a syllable, and

helps you to see patterns in words.

It is particularly useful if used in conjunction with the next technique.

Adapting the pronunciation

While syllabification is useful for words that are spelt as they sound, some 30% of English words that adults use are not spelt according to their sound pattern. Some of these words can be tackled by adapting your pronunciation to emphasise their spelling patterns.

Exaggerate the pronunciation of the difficult part.

describe (stress 'des')

covered (stress 'ed' ending)

hostage (stress 'age' ending)

Emphasise each syllable.

li/bra/ry

def/in/ite

Sound out the silent letters.

knock

ledge

listen

Rules

Learning spelling rules can be useful as it is easier and quicker to learn words in groups which follow a pattern, than to learn each word individually. Later in this chapter you will be shown some of the most helpful rules.

Mnemonics

These are the memory devices that can be used to help you to learn and remember spellings.

e.g. 'rr' and 'ss' in emba**rr**a**ss** can be remembered by '**two red** cheeks and **two scarlet** ears'.

Here are some useful spelling memory aids.

Grouping similar words into memorable phrases or sentences.

e.g. Carg**oes** of potat**oes** and tomat**oes**.

Rhymes

e.g. for 'ei' spellings:

    The wicked bandit

    Who practised dec**ei**t

    Gazed at the c**ei**ling

    And s**ei**zed the rec**ei**pt

Word pairs with

    a similar spelling pattern;

EXAMPLES:

br**ui**sed fr**ui**t

a s**ou**p c**ou**pon

    or a different pattern.

EXAMPLES:

famil**iar** but not sim**ilar**

se**par**ate not des**per**ate

Acronyms

e.g.

sigh

Sid is Greta's hero

A careful attitude

In order to improve your spelling you need to adopt a careful attitude.

▶ When copying words from a dictionary, take care to copy correctly – there is no point in learning an incorrectly spelt word.

▶ Final copies should be correct – first drafts can contain errors as you will be concentrating on putting your ideas down on paper, not on spelling.

▶ Proof-read your writing carefully – read it critically and look for mistakes. Carefully check any words you are uncertain about.

Spelling and writing

In Chapter 1 we stressed that the degree of accuracy required of your spelling will depend upon the task. If you are writing purely for your own pleasure accuracy is not so important, but formal writing tasks require correct spelling. You can help yourself to achieve this by:

> using a dictionary;

> careful proof-reading.

Using a dictionary

At some time you will need to check a spelling in a dictionary. **Always attempt to spell the word before you check it in a dictionary**. This will allow you to develop your confidence – if you keep referring to a dictionary as you write, you will begin to doubt your spelling ability. Use a dictionary after you have proof-read your rough draft and identified all the problematical words.

You may find using a dictionary difficult, but you can make using one less of a chore by:

> being aware of its contents and the symbols it uses,

> being confident about alphabetical order,

> using the guide words to help you locate the correct page,

> familiarising yourself with the arrangement of the information beneath each word,

> and knowing about quartiles.

If you place a dictionary on its spine it will fall open into two halves, at about the letter M. In the same way, divide each half into half again and the pages will probably fall open at E and at S.

The quartiles are

A – E
F – M
N – S
T – Z

If you use this technique to find the correct quartile, it will speed up your search for words.

Using a dictionary efficiently at the correct stage in the writing process will increase your confidence and skill.

Proof-reading

It is advisable to proof-read your writing twice – once after the rough or first draft and again when you have completed the final copy. Check once again for spelling mistakes as you will then be able to concentrate on this one aspect of your writing.

Checking for spelling errors is primarily a visual skill – you will be identifying words that look wrong.

** Check this memo for spelling errors.

MEMORANDUM

To: All staff

From: Personel Manager   **Date:** 8 September 1992

Subject: Thefts from cars

Their have been sevral instences of thefts from cars parked in Car Park A (Ewell Road) resently. The securty officer has aranged for gaurds to make peroidic checks but your help is also required. Please insure your car is left locked and any valuble articles are put out of site in the boot. Report any suspicous insidents to Mr Hallant (cheif security officer).

Some people lack confidence in their ability to learn and check words visually so they have to adopt other strategies.

| knowing and understanding rules | knowing possible and probable letter combinations | being aware of homophones |

62

Rules

You may think that English spelling is illogical or that rules aren't reliable, but some rules can be useful to know as they cover a large number of words and have few exceptions.

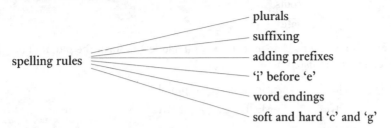

spelling rules
- plurals
- suffixing
- adding prefixes
- 'i' before 'e'
- word endings
- soft and hard 'c' and 'g'

Plurals

5

▶ Most nouns form the plural by adding 's'.

EXAMPLES:

singular	plural
sweet	sweets
brick	bricks
alternator	alternators

▶ Nouns which end in ch, sh, s, ss, x, z or zz add 'es' to form the plural.

EXAMPLES:

singular	plural
address	addresses
pitch	pitches
mess	messes

▶ To form the plural of nouns ending in y, look at the letter before the 'y'. If there is a consonant before the 'y', change 'y' to 'i' and add 'es'. If there is a vowel before 'y', just add 's' to the word.

EXAMPLES:

singular	plural
family	families
factory	factories
relay	relays
chimney	chimneys

▶ Most nouns which end in 'f' or 'fe' add 's' to form the plural.

EXAMPLES:

singular	plural
roof	roofs
safe	safes

However, a few nouns change 'f' to 'v' and add 'es' to form the plural. The most common are listed here.

singular	plural	singular	plural
self	selves	shelf	shelves
thief	thieves	loaf	loaves
leaf	leaves	knife	knives*
wife	wives*	life	lives*
half	halves		

*Note: 's' not 'es' is added to these words.

▶ Most nouns that end in 'o' add 's' to form the plural:

EXAMPLES:

singular	plural
radio	radios
shampoo	shampoos
solo	solos

but a few need 'es' to form the plural.

EXAMPLES:

singular	plural	singular	plural
potato	potatoes	tomato	tomatoes
hero	heroes	cargo	cargoes

** Write the plurals of these words.

computer	alley	box	pansy
tannoy	studio	stitch	wish
church	copy	proof	suffix

Suffixing

A suffix is a letter or syllable added to the end of a word.

word   suffix

walk + er ⟶ walker

clean + est ⟶ cleanest

switch + ing ⟶ switching.

Doubling rule

When a suffix beginning with a **vowel** or a **'y'** is added to a word containing:

one syllable,

one short vowel, and

one final consonant,

the final consonant is doubled.

EXAMPLES:

drip ⟨ one syllable / one short vowel (i) / one final consonant (p) add 'ing' – dripping

chat ⟨ one syllable / one short vowel (a) / one final consonant (t) add 'y' – chatty

Silent 'e' rule

If a word ends in a **silent e**, this 'e' is dropped when a vowel suffix or 'y' is added.

EXAMPLES:

word   suffix

come + ing ⟶ coming

waste + ed ⟶ wasted

haze + y ⟶ hazy

But some words retain the 'e'.

EXAMPLES:

word   suffix

dye + ing ⟶ dyeing

manage + able ⟶ manageable (See soft and hard 'c' and 'g' rules.)

A few words can be spelt with or without the 'e'.

e.g. sizable or sizeable

'y' to 'i' rule

When a suffix is added to a word which **ends in a consonant before a final y**, change 'y' to 'i'. (Except when adding the suffix 'ing'.)

word	suffix	
heavenly	+ ness	⟶ heavenliness
steady	+ ed	⟶ steadied

'l' rule

In **two-syllable words** which **end in 'l'** and have a vowel before that 'l', double the final 'l' when adding a vowel or 'y' suffix.

EXAMPLES:

word	suffix	
cancel	+ ing	⟶ cancelling
expel	+ ed	⟶ expelled

There are a few exceptions.

EXAMPLES:

word	suffix	
legal	+ ity	⟶ legality
formal	+ ise	⟶ formalise

Two-syllable words

When adding a vowel or 'y' suffix to a two-syllable word **where the stress falls on the second syllable,** double the final consonant.

EXAMPLES:

word	suffix	
commit	+ ing	⟶ committing
refer	+ al	⟶ referral

This rule can be difficult to use as it relies upon your ability to hear where the stress falls in a word. If this is so, you can either try writing the word both ways and then choose which looks right, or you can check the word in a dictionary.

'ic' words

When adding the suffixes **ing, er, ed** or y to words which end in 'ic', add 'k' to the base word.

EXAMPLES:

word	suffix	
panic	+ y	⟶ panicky
mimic	+ ing	⟶ mimicking

When adding **ly** to words ending in 'ic', add 'al' to the base word.

EXAMPLES:

word	suffix	
fantastic	+ ly	⟶ fantastically
basic	+ ly	⟶ basically

Prefixes

A prefix is a group of letters added to the beginning of a word to change the meaning of the word.

When a prefix is added to a word, usually no alteration is made to the spelling of the word or the prefix.

prefix	word	
un	+ happy	⟶ unhappy
dis	+ satisfy	⟶ dissatisfy

When the prefix 'all' or 'well' is added, one 'l' is dropped. e.g. altogether

(And note those words where the prefix 'well' is linked by a hyphen to the base word. e.g. well-made, well-off.)

'i' before 'e' rule

Do you know the *complete* rule?

'i' before 'e' except after 'c' but only in words where these letters make a long e sound.

EXAMPLES:

achieve

niece

receive

conceit

If the letters make a different sound, the spelling is 'ei'.

EXAMPLES:

neighbour (long a sound)

leisure (short e sound)

weir ('ear' sound)

heir ('air' sound)

height (long i sound)

Exceptions are:

seize   counterfeit   protein   caffeine

– all of which are pronounced with a long e sound but spelt 'ei'.

Word endings

As the voice often trails off at the end of words, it can be difficult to distinguish the final sound of a word.

There are a few rules that may help you.

'al' or 'le'?

If you are uncertain about whether a word ends 'cal' or 'cle', think about the function of the word in the sentence.

Words which end in **cal** are **adjectives** (describing words); words which end in **cle** are **nouns** (naming words).

e.g. Henry is very <u>musical</u>.

adjective (describing Henry)

The **vehicle** is designed to hold four people.

noun

'le' or 'cl'?

Certain endings <u>do not occur</u> in English.

   mle

   nle

   rle

   vle

   wle

An 'ul' sound after 'm', 'n', 'r', 'v' or 'w' is usually **el**.

camel

panel

quarrel

gravel

trowel

'tion', 'sion' or 'ssion'?

All these are possible endings for the 'shun' sound. The majority of words ending in a 'shun' sound are spelt **tion**.

e.g. attention

'ance' or 'ence'?

These endings are quite difficult to distinguish, but words that end in 'ant' generally take the suffix **ance** and those that end 'ent' become **ence**. (The 'ant' and 'ent' endings are usually easier to hear.)

EXAMPLES:

ignorant	ignorance
dissonant	dissonance
diffident	diffidence
convenient	convenience

'cede', 'ceed' or 'sede'?

All three combinations sound the same but the majority of words ending in this sound take the **cede** spelling.

e.g. intercede

The most common **ceed** words are proceed, exceed and succeed.

The only word ending in **sede** is supersede.

'ise' or 'ize'?

These sound the same and often either ending is acceptable.

e.g. dramatise ✓

    dramatize ✓

ise is the commoner ending so, if in doubt, it may be better to choose 'ise' but a few words <u>must</u> end 'ize'.

EXAMPLES:

size

capsize

Soft and hard 'c' and 'g' sounds

'c' and 'g' usually make a soft sound when they are followed by 'e', 'i' or 'y'.

EXAMPLES:

central	specify	cylinder
regenerate	gigantic	dingy

but there are a number of quite common words in which 'g' followed by 'e' or 'i' has a hard sound.

EXAMPLES:

get	girl	giggle

'c' and 'g' usually make a hard sound when they are followed by 'a', 'o', 'u' or a consonant.

EXAMPLES:

camp	welcome	cutlery	cramp	enclose
engage	gone	guarantee	glimpse	granular

In words ending 'ce' or 'ge', the final 'e' is retained to keep the 'c' or 'g' soft when the suffixes 'able', 'ade' or 'ous' are added. These words do <u>not</u> follow the normal suffixing rule for silent 'e' words.

EXAMPLES:

word	suffix	
change + able	→	changeable
notice + able	→	noticeable
courage + ous	→	courageous
orange + ade	→	orangeade

Possible and probable letter combinations

It is estimated that about 85% of English words follow a pattern or obey a rule. You have already seen many occasions where you can apply a rule to help you spell or check a word. By being aware of possible and probable letter combinations, you can:

more accurately guess at the spelling of a word;

use the knowledge to help you proof-read for spelling errors;

find possible alternative spellings for a word you have tried to check in a dictionary but have been unable to find.

There are some sounds in English that can be made by a variety of letter combinations.

e.g. an 'or' sound can be made by

We could say that 'or', 'au', 'aw' are all <u>possible</u> combinations, but 'or' is the <u>probable</u> combination as it occurs in words more frequently than the other two combinations. If 'or' isn't the correct choice then you could apply the following guidelines.

▶ 'au' mostly occurs at the beginning and in the middle of words.

EXAMPLES:

audience

audacious

caution

▶ 'aw' generally occurs at the end of words.

e.g. outlaw

▶ 'au' rarely occurs at the end of words.

If you are in doubt about the spelling of a word,

write the word using all the <u>possible</u> letter combinations you can think of,

decide which looks right,

consider whether it is the <u>probable</u> letter combination (think of similar words).

Check your attempts against the dictionary.

** Read the advice on possible and probable letter combinations for the 'ur' sound and then complete the words.

(Possible combinations are 'ur' 'ir' 'er' and 'ear'.

'er' often occurs at the end of words,

'ur' is more common than 'ir', and

'ear' is used least.)

s...geon	th...st	c...cle
suff...	s...vive	...nest
f...niture	p...chase	...ly
sub...b	m...g...	...gent

Homophones

These are words that sound the same but are spelt differently and have different meanings. Confusion can arise when the wrong word is chosen for the context.

e.g.

The <u>crews</u> helped Ashefa to recover from her illness. ✗

The <u>cruise</u> helped Ashefa to recover from her illness. ✓

These are some common homophones. You may find it helpful to check the meaning of any you are uncertain about.

miner/minor	heir/air
dependent/dependant	sheer/shear
story/storey	piece/peace
cereal/serial	shoot/chute
board/bored	compliment/complement
ceiling/sealing	shore/sure
principle/principal	council/counsel
currant/current	weight/wait

There are other pairs of words that can also be confused as they have a similar, although not the same, sound.

EXAMPLES:

elicit	illicit
affect	effect
eminent	imminent
liable	libel
personal	personnel

By being aware of homophones and other confusing pairs of words, your proof-reading may be more effective.

Final thoughts

We hope that this chapter has provided an insight into some techniques and strategies which can be used to help overcome spelling difficulties. Obviously in one chapter we cannot give detailed guidance, but if you feel that you need more help with spelling you will find the book *Getting to Grips with Spelling* useful.

Spelling is important but there is no point in learning long lists of words devised by someone who has no knowledge of you or your needs. **Learn the words which you think will be of most benefit to you.** The only purpose in improving your spelling is so that you can write more effectively and confidently.

6
Vocabulary

Whether we are speaking or writing, we convey our messages in words. Words are the medium through which we express our thoughts, feelings, ideas, questions, remarks, etc.

If we are conveying our message orally, we may use body language or tones of voice to help us create a clearer or more vivid picture. We can also assess whether our listeners have understood by watching their facial expressions or by asking questions. However, when we write we have to rely entirely on the words we use to express the message correctly, clearly and appropriately. Obviously, to communicate successfully in writing we need a large and varied vocabulary so that we can select the most effective words for our purpose and audience.

A large and varied vocabulary allows you to:

▶ express your ideas precisely	by choosing the exact word;
▶ express your ideas concisely	by expressing your ideas in the most direct language;
▶ use the appropriate tone	by choosing the most suitable words to reflect the degree of formality;
▶ use a range of writing styles	by choosing the correct vocabulary for your style;
▶ write with confidence and ease	by feeling comfortable with the situation – knowing you have suitable words at your fingertips.

In this chapter we will consider:

how you can develop a varied vocabulary,

how you can make your writing vivid,

formal and informal vocabulary,

which words to avoid when writing, and

how proof-reading can help eliminate inaccurate, imprecise or dull words from your writing.

Developing your vocabulary

It is estimated that the average person's vocabulary contains 15,000–20,000 words. While this is adequate for most everyday needs there will undoubtedly be occasions when we feel dissatisfied with the words we have used in our writing. Perhaps they have not created a sufficiently vivid image, or have not conveyed our exact ideas.

The size of our vocabulary is not fixed; it can be extended to accommodate changes in our lives, for example a new interest, a new job or a course of training could cause your vocabulary to expand. Indeed, your vocabulary will continue to grow throughout your life if you encourage it to do so.

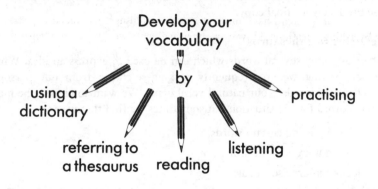

Using a dictionary

A good dictionary is an essential tool for any writer but it will only be effective if you use it confidently and competently. A good dictionary will help you develop your writing skills by:

▶ providing you with the precise meanings of words which you wish to use in your writing but are uncertain about,

▶ indicating the part of speech of each entry, so helping you to use the word correctly in a sentence,

▶ allowing you to check the spelling of a word, and

▶ giving some synonyms and related words and phrases which widen your choice of words.

▶ Avoid cheap 'special purchase' dictionaries which will probably be inadequate for your writing needs.

▶ It is worth spending some time familiarising yourself with the arrangement, layout and symbols used in your dictionary. You will then find your dictionary easier and quicker to use.

▶ It is advisable to consult your dictionary after you have finished your first draft. If you keep stopping while you write to check your spelling or the exact meaning of a word, or to select a more appropriate word, you will find your writing lacks fluency. Instead, underline any words which you are uncertain about and refer to a dictionary during the editing stage before you produce your final copy.

Referring to a thesaurus

There are often several words which can be used to express an idea. While we are writing we are frequently making a choice from our personal storehouse of words – our natural vocabulary. We want to choose the most suitable word for the situation but sometimes we find that we are:

> repeatedly using certain words,
>
> choosing uninteresting words, or
>
> selecting imprecise words.

At such times we can refer to a thesaurus or a dictionary of synonyms for a wider selection of possible synonyms, related words and antonyms.

There are two main types of thesauruses: alphabetically arranged thesauruses and editions based on *Roget's Thesaurus*.

We have found that most students prefer using the former as the alphabetical arrangement means that it is easier and quicker to refer to. (A dictionary of synonyms is likely to provide a more limited choice of alternatives than a thesaurus.)

You may wonder whether it is necessary to have a thesaurus as well as a general English dictionary, but they do complement each other. While a dictionary sometimes provides a few synonyms, a thesaurus will provide a greater number of possible alternative words under each entry. A thesaurus will not give any definitions for the words it lists, so you may need to refer to a dictionary to check the meaning of any unfamiliar words.

** Using a thesaurus and a dictionary, choose words which could replace those underlined in this passage.

> The grey November day drew to a close. The grey mist which had hung around all day stopped the last weak traces of sunlight from penetrating the gloom.
>
> John walked along the streets, trampling through piles of wet leaves. His mood matched the gloomy weather – he was miserable, cold and tired. He thought of his home in Rarotonga: the strong heat of the sun, the waves breaking on the coral reef and the long beaches of silver sand edged by tall palm trees. It was an island paradise and he had swapped it for a college course in Britain!

Reading

By reading sufficiently demanding books, magazines and newspapers, you will encounter a variety of unfamiliar words. If you make an effort to incorporate these words into your natural vocabulary you will be able to use them in your writing. The procedure outlined overleaf may seem tedious but active reading is the most effective way to develop your vocabulary.

Create a personal dictionary

If you are serious about developing your vocabulary, you will need to record your newly acquired words and their definitions. You can use an alphabetically arranged book, a card file or a computer file to store your new words and their meanings, usage, synonyms etc.

> Plausible –
>   seemingly worthy of approval or praise
>   fair spoken
>   e.g. a plausible remark
>
> Synonyms: glib, ingratiating, specious

Underline the
unfamiliar word.

Continue reading but
return to the underlined
word at a suitable break
in the text.

Try to guess the meaning
of the word from the rest
of the sentence — the context.

Check the meaning of the word
in a dictionary.

Note down the meaning or
meanings of the word
and its correct spelling
in your personal dictionary.

Practice using the new word
until it becomes a part
of your natural vocabulary.

Listening

A child learns new words by listening to other people. He or she will imitate the sound of the word and practise using it in a variety of ways until it is firmly fixed in the memory. You can continue to increase your vocabulary by active listening through adulthood.

Whenever you listen to the radio or television, you are exposed to other people's vocabulary. If you take sufficient notice of the way people express themselves, you will discover new words. By noting down these new words to research and practise later, you will utilise a valuable vocabulary resource.

Practising

Your personal dictionary will provide you with a permanent record of your target words – those words which could, with sufficient practice, become part of your natural vocabulary.

6

▶ Test yourself on the meanings and spellings of new words.

▶ Write the words in a variety of sentences – this will allow you to appreciate the various functions the words perform in different contexts.

▶ Use the words in conversation – you may prefer to practise on your family and friends first!

** Find a magazine or newspaper article on an unfamiliar subject. Read it, underlining any words you would not normally use in your speech or writing. Follow the procedure outlined in this chapter for researching and practising these words.

Vivid writing

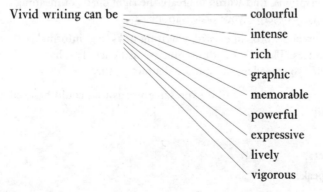

Vivid writing can be
colourful
intense
rich
graphic
memorable
powerful
expressive
lively
vigorous

Such writing creates powerful images which attempt to convey the writer's own experiences, thoughts and feelings. The writer will have chosen words with care, avoiding faded words (e.g. big, old, pretty) and predictable, obvious phrases (e.g. a nice, warm bath; a happy ending).

Consider how Susan Hill in *The Magic Apple Tree* describes the start of autumn.

> There are wasps droning about all over the fallen fruit at my feet. There is a dew on the grass so thick that it seems to have rained heavily in the night. Across the bramble bush that has grown up from the field on the other side of the low stone wall and begun to scramble over it, cobwebs are strung about, delicate, tingling with tiny, tiny drops of moisture, silver as mercury beads.

When we read such passages we can picture the scene in our imagination – the words may recall our own observations and memories of autumn mornings. As you can see from the passage, it is not always necessary to choose long, complicated words to create a powerful image.

When we are talking we can't spend time choosing the most apt or descriptive words, but writing provides us with the time to select our words.

Helpful Hints

▶ When you are writing, make an effort to select unusual words: don't just opt for the same words that you would use when speaking.

▶ Use a thesaurus to find vivid alternatives to faded, overused words.

▶ Be aware of the words other writers use to express their ideas. Collect unusual or striking examples and try to incorporate them into your writing.

▶ When writing decriptions, find words to create the right shade of meaning – words that precisely describe your observations.

▶ Use colourful or precise words in everyday writing tasks, e.g. informal letters or diary entries. This allows you to practise using less familiar words and provides your reader with a more distinct picture.

** Using a thesaurus and dictionary find expressive words that could be used in a description of:

> a wet night;
>
> a cherished pet;
>
> an effective speaker;
>
> an overgrown garden.

Formal and informal vocabulary

You have already seen that in writing we rely principally upon our choice of words to create the correct tone.

EXAMPLES:

1 I was <u>upset</u> by your <u>cheeky comeback</u>.

    suggests distress rather than anger   conversational, informal words

2 I was <u>disgusted</u> by your <u>flippant response</u>.

    suggests anger   more formal language

Sentence 1 has an informal tone; in sentence 2 the tone conveys a greater degree of seriousness and anger.

Either sentence may be correct according to the situation. You must consider:

> the purpose for writing,
>
> the audience, and
>
> the formality required.

We usually find it easier to choose the correct words for informal situations. Why?

> We feel more relaxed with people we know well.
>
> We spend more of our time in informal situations than in formal situations.
>
> If we are writing an informal letter or note, we can use words from our everyday language and can, perhaps, be less precise.

Formal situations require formal language. Formal writing tasks require the greatest care and effort as they provide a permanent record and can influence other people's impressions of us and our abilities.

Helpful Hints

▶ Be aware of formal words and phrases. You will find that chapters in Section 2 provide you with examples of formal language and writing tasks.

▶ Find examples of well-written formal letters, reports, etc. Study the way the writer has expressed his or her ideas. Note down helpful words and phrases that are relevant to your needs.

6

▶ Writing formal language does not entail the use of pompous, complicated, over-long words. You should avoid:

colloquial words or phrases

EXAMPLES:

I think we <u>got that a bit wrong</u>.

   could be replaced by:

I think we <u>made a mistake</u>.

He is <u>into</u> classical music.

   could be rewritten:

He is <u>interested</u> in classical music

exaggerated or meaningless words

e.g. He is <u>terribly</u> rich. (Omit 'terribly'.)

verbose language or 'officialese'

e.g. I wish to respectfully remind you of our years of faithful service to your company... .

   could be replaced by:

I would like to remind you that for many years we have provided a service to your company... .

jargon

Unless you are writing for an audience which shares your interests or experiences, avoid technical words and phrases which might confuse the general reader.

For formal writing, simple and direct language is the most effective means of communication.

Proof-reading

In Chapter 1 you were shown the importance of proof-reading and editing. You may find it necessary to make a separate check for vocabulary.

▶ As you proof-read your first draft, underline:

   inappropriate words

   repetitive words

   imprecise and vague words

   dull words

▶ After identifying such words, you can use your thesaurus and dictionary to find more vivid or suitable words to replace them.

▶ When you proof-read you may also find words that you have misused, perhaps because you have confused them with a similar sounding word.

e.g. 'accept' for 'except'. (Chapter 5 provides more examples of homophones – words which sound the same.)

▶ In an examination it isn't possible to produce a first draft but you should be prepared to proof-read your writing and replace inexact vocabulary. If you are producing writing for a coursework folder, don't be too easily satisfied.

▶ Writing can never be perfect; there is often a more effective way of expressing your ideas. Time spent on editing and improving your writing may be rewarded by a higher mark.

Final thoughts

The words you use in your writing are important and the amount of care you put into choosing the right word will be evident to your reader. By developing your vocabulary you will derive more pleasure from writing and feel more confident about it. More detailed guidance on vocabulary can be found in the vocabulary book in this series.

6

7

Gathering and Organising Ideas

Perhaps the two most difficult aspects of writing are knowing what to write and how to start. When faced with a writing task, you might sit and look at a blank piece of paper feeling devoid of ideas. However, by knowing how to gather ideas and organise them into a plan before you begin writing you will:

feel more confident about the writing process,

spend less time waiting for inspiration, and

concentrate on imparting your message effectively as you will have already established the framework.

In Chapter 1 we referred to the purpose behind any piece of writing.

Why are you writing?

What do you want your writing to achieve?

Asking yourself these questions is a good way of approaching the task of gathering ideas.

Identifying the purpose for writing should also indicate how much planning and organisation is required for the task.

Formal writing tasks

Most plans for formal writing tasks will follow this pattern:

▶ **introduction** (outlines the reason for writing)

▶ **development** (forms the body of the piece of writing and develops the theme)

▶ **conclusion** (sums up the writer's ideas)

If you are writing a timed essay in an exam, it is essential to set aside some time for planning as you will then find the essay:

is easier to write,

has a better structure,

includes all the points you wish to make, and thus creates a better impression on the examiner.

In this chapter we will be looking at how to develop and organise ideas for four different writing tasks.

Letters

Essays

Factual writing

Personal writing

Letters

Informal letter writing

Even if you don't have many opportunities for writing formal or business letters, you will probably have written a considerable number of informal letters to friends and relatives. Although such letters may not require the careful planning of formal letters, it is still helpful to consider your purpose for writing before you start. For example, you may be writing in reply to a letter you have received and need to respond to several points.

Obviously, not all informal letters are written as replies; we also write informal letters to:

give information,

offer opinions,

maintain a relationship,

describe events, or

offer help.

Careful planning can be useful for those informal letters that you find difficult, particularly if you are uncertain about how to begin the letter or how to express your thoughts. Before writing such letters it may be necessary to jot down your ideas and then arrange them in an acceptable order: this will allow you to concentrate on choosing the most appropriate language and style for the task.

Think of planning a letter as being similar to writing a shopping list where you list the items you want and then group them together in the order you will shop for them.

Read this letter.

6 Holme View,
Longsight,
Manchester,
M8 3JK
24 August 1992

Dear Sue,

I hope you are now feeling better. I expect that now you've had some time at home to recover, and have been able to sit outside in the sunshine, you're looking and feeling stronger.

We do miss you at work and look forward to your return. There have been several changes since you went into hospital: John Lacy has retired (lucky man!) and Nigel has taken over John's job. He is finding it quite difficult to cope and is hoping that you will come back soon so you can rescue him from the muddle.

I thought you might be interested in the book I'm sending you with this letter. I saw it in Smith's and thought it might amuse you – I know you've always wanted to live in France. Peter Mayle makes it sound fun but hard work. Anyway, I hope you enjoy it and find some time to read it before you return.

Take care of yourself and do let me know when I can visit you again.

Yours,
Peggy

Sue might list these points to mention in her reply to Peggy.

feeling better
changes at work
thanks for book/letter
visit

She may then add two points she wishes to make.

back to work in 4 weeks
going away for a few days

Having identified all the points she wishes to make, Sue might number the points in the order she will tackle them.

2 feeling better
6 changes at work
1 thanks for book and letter
4 visit
5 back to work in four weeks
3 going away for a few days

This is how her final letter might read.

2 Western Road,
Levenshulme
Manchester. M13 5JH
27 August 1992

Dear Peggy,

Thank you very much for your letter. It was lovely to hear from you and thank you for the book as well. I'm already half-way through it and enjoying every page.

I'm sure you'll be pleased to hear that I'm feeling much better than when you last saw me and I'm looking quite fit and healthy now.

The lovely weather has encouraged me to go away for a few days next week but I hope you will come and see me before I go. As I'm here all the time, I suggest you phone me and let me know when it is convenient for you.

The doctor reckons I should be able to go back to work in four weeks' time if I continue to make good progress. However, having heard about Nigel having John's old job, I'm not sure that I want to!

Please phone soon and arrange a day when you can come over. I am looking forward to seeing you and hearing all the office gossip. Thank you once again for the book and for writing.

Love,
Sue

** Try organising the 'shopping list' of ideas below in a logical and acceptable order. You are writing to a friend to describe your move to a new town.

come and see new flat

still sorting out

removal men arrived early

arrived at new flat – no key

rained all day

town very busy after life in a village

new neighbours very pleasant and helpful

not enough boxes to pack belongings

still lose my way getting to work

good shopping and night life

Formal letter writing

In the section on informal letters, you were shown how you could gather ideas by identifying the points you wish to reply to and creating a 'shopping list' of ideas. In formal letter writing, which requires a higher degree of accuracy and precision, such planning is essential.

Study the letter below, noting the points which have been underlined.

DERBY LOCAL HISTORY SOCIETY

Chairman:	Secretary:	Treasurer:
Mrs B. Ward	Mr E. Turner	Ms C. Rafferty
	46 Goodison Avenue	
	Hinley	
	Derby DY6 4RB	

5th December 1992

Dear Member,

As you will recall, at our last meeting it was proposed that our society should hold a 'History of Derby' exhibition in the Central Library. The committee has arranged for this exhibition to be held on 22 February 1993 from 10.30 am to 4.00 pm.

It is hoped that there will be a display of materials relating to the history of our city. If you are able to loan photographs, documents, etc., this would be much appreciated. Please indicate whether you will allow copies to be made of any of your material. We are also hoping to include a display of articles made in Derby. Contributions to this display would also be gratefully received. Please mark the articles with your name.

We have been promised help from the library staff but also require assistance from our members, either during the exhibition or with the setting up and dismantling of the exhibits.

I would be grateful if you could write to me, outlining any assistance you could provide to help our society make this a successful event.

Yours sincerely,

Edward Turner

Edward Turner (Secretary)

If you had received this letter and marked the points you wished to respond to, you could then list your responses.

have some photos - High Street and Corporation Street in 1908

newspaper cuttings - Derby Recorder 1940-1945

nothing made in Derby

could help before 10.00 am setting up exhibition

The plan for this letter could be:

Paragraph 1: thank you for letter – sounds very interesting – can offer some support (**introduction**)

Paragraph 2: can lend photos, cuttings – can make copies of photos – unfortunately no articles made in Derby (**development**)

Paragraph 3: could help with setting up – unavailable after 10.00 am – work commitments (**development**)

Paragraph 4: please contact me about where and when to send materials and if you need my help (**conclusion**)

** Using the plan given above, write your reply to the secretary of the society. If you are unsure about the layout of your letter, refer to Chapter 9.

If you aren't replying to a letter, you may have to think more carefully about why you are writing and what you want your letter to achieve before you start listing the points you wish to make.

EXAMPLE:

You wish to write to a manufacturer to complain about a kettle you bought six months ago. The cut-out switch has failed on a number of occasions. Although it has been repaired twice, it is still faulty, so you want your money refunded.

Consider your purpose: to complain about the kettle and to obtain a refund.

<u>Consider what other information is required</u> to support your argument:

  details of purchase;

  details of previous repairs;

  other information (enclosing receipt, returning kettle, etc.).

The information to be included in the letter could be arranged in this order:

<u>Paragraph 1</u>: details of purchase and nature of complaint (**introduction**)

<u>Paragraph 2</u>: brief details of repairs (**development**)

<u>Paragraph 3</u>: returning kettle, enclosing receipt – would like a refund (**conclusion**)

A detailed, well-organised plan will help you to impart your message effectively in a formal or business letter.

Essays

It is unlikely that you will be required to write a formal essay unless you are following an academic course. However, some of the ways of gathering and organising information which are shown in this section on essays can be applied to other writing tasks.

Essays can be

descriptive

narrative

discursive

Descriptive essays

Essays which require you to describe a person, place or emotion lend themselves to the 'spider approach'.

EXAMPLE:

You are asked to write a description of a person you know well and like.

You choose your subject and think about the various aspects you might consider in your description.

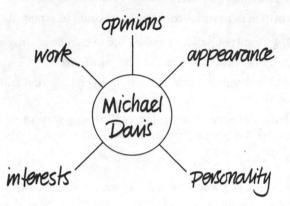

You list your ideas under each heading.

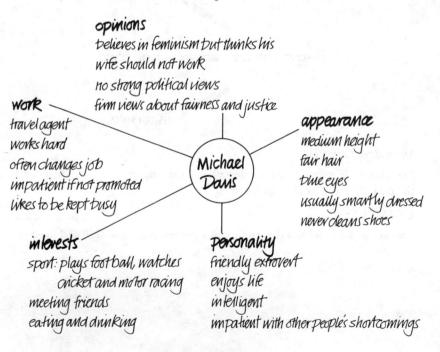

Step 3

You decide how you will present these ideas in your essay. This essay could be tackled in two ways.

Each aspect of the person could be described in turn;

Some aspects could be described and others could be shown by providing examples to illustrate them. You could expand the 'spider' by adding these examples:

7

opinions
believes in feminism but thinks his
wife should not work
no strong political views
firm views about fairness and justice

last year's
'disagreement'
with police

work
travel agent
works hard
often changes job
impatient if not promoted
likes to be kept busy

Michael
Davis

appearance
medium height
fair hair
blue eyes
usually smartly dressed
never cleans shoes

interests
sport: plays football, watches
cricket and motor racing
meeting friends
eating and drinking

personality
friendly extrovert
enjoys life
intelligent
impatient with other people's shortcomings

Paul's wedding

Vietnamese food
describe meal last
saturday night

least fit member of
team—hasn't finished
a match yet!

attitude to
indecisive clients

Step 4

Having assembled all your ideas, arrange them in the order you feel is most appropriate and most likely to produce an interesting essay. You will probably find that each aspect forms a separate paragraph of writing.

** Create a 'spider' to generate ideas about a place you have enjoyed visiting. Use these ideas as starting points.

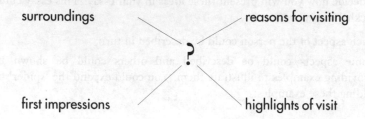

surroundings

reasons for visiting

?

first impressions

highlights of visit

Narrative essays

In this type of essay you either create an imaginary story or recount a real event. Your essay may include some descriptive passages to create atmosphere and effect but the main content will be the story.

As the essay charts a period of time it may be useful to assemble your ideas in a flow chart.

EXAMPLE:

You are asked to write about 'A First Day'. This may be a first day at school, college, work or any other first day. You decide to write about your first day at work, when you were employed as a Saturday assistant in a chain store. Your plan follows the events of the day.

journey there

arrival – met the
personnel manager

taken down onto shop
floor – met the staff

shown how to operate the
till – told about duties

morning passed slowly –
very quiet

lunch

afternoon busy – made
several mistakes

5.30 pm – felt exhausted
tidied section – received
wages

Having considered your outline plan, you feel that certain aspects need more description so you add ideas which you can develop further in your essay in order to make it more interesting and detailed.

journey there	— I was apprehensive in case I was late.
arrival - met the Personnel manager	— an intimidating interview I felt tongue-tied and stupid.
taken down onto shop floor - met staff	— It seemed strange to be on the other side of the counter - a new perspective on the shop.
shown how to operate till - told about duties	— working a till is more difficult than it looks!
morning passed slowly very quiet	— I tried to look busy, but wanted to escape.
lunch	— Freedom!
afternoon busy - made several mistakes	— I still had problems with the till - some customers became irate. I was embarrassed, but time passed in a flash.
5.30pm - felt exhausted tidied section - received wages	— My head throbbed and feet ached but I was elated when paid.

You will notice that the more developed plan not only recounts what happened but also records the feelings and attitudes of the person, which gives a more detailed and interesting impression of the day.

You would probably write about this topic in chronological order, but you could describe your day through a series of flashbacks, not necessarily recounting the details in the order they occurred.

** Devise a plan for an essay in which you recount your experiences about a disastrous holiday (real or imagined).

Discursive essays

In these essays you are required to express your opinion on a subject. (e.g. How can we conserve the environment for future generations?)

Or you may be asked to present conflicting points of view. (e.g. Vegetarianism is the only sensible diet. Discuss.)

The planning process is <u>crucial</u> in this type of essay; without a detailed plan, it is easy to drift away from the topic or fail to develop the topic sufficiently.

If you have the opportunity, it is advisable to research the subject before you begin the planning stages. When you feel you have sufficient information to write about the subject, you can begin to organise your ideas. If your essay requires you to present both points of view on a subject, it may be helpful to list the points you wish to make under two headings – <u>pros</u> and <u>cons</u> (or <u>for</u> and <u>against</u>).

EXAMPLE:

Vegetarianism is the only sensible diet. Discuss.

<u>pros</u>	<u>cons</u>
Vegetables are often cheaper than meat and can encourage more creative cooking.	Vegetable dishes tend to be bland and perhaps require more skilful cooking than meat. Vegetarianism is not our traditional diet and to adopt it we need to learn new skills.
Vegetarianism doesn't require the slaughter of animals.	If everyone were vegetarian, farm animals would face extinction.
There would be no need for cruel, intensive animal farming if more people became vegetarian.	It is possible to raise and slaughter animals humanely and we could concentrate on developing these methods.
Vegetarianism is a healthier diet than eating meat.	A mixed diet of meat and vegetables provides sufficient protein and vitamins for a healthy diet. It is possible to buy lean meat and remove most of the fat.
Vegetarians are not affected by health scares, e.g. BSE and salmonella.	Some animals would still be raised and killed for their skin and fur, e.g. for leather shoes.

Having generated the two lists, you can decide how to group the ideas and organise the essay.

Suggested plan

It is usually easier to present the arguments for one side then develop the opposing views and, if appropriate, finally make your personal standpoint clear.

<u>Introduction</u> Vegetarianism is gaining in popularity – meat-eating is an issue which provokes strong feelings.

<u>Development</u> Present one side of the argument, with evidence where necessary. Use the first point, about cooking, as the pivotal point to link the two halves of the essay together.

<u>Conclusion</u> On the strength of the arguments presented, come down on one side or the other, or, if appropriate, present and justify your personal view.

If you are required only to present your own opinion on a subject, you may find it easier to generate ideas if you 'brainstorm'.

EXAMPLE

You have been given as your subject 'How can we conserve the environment for future generations?' After 'brainstorming' the issue, these are your ideas.

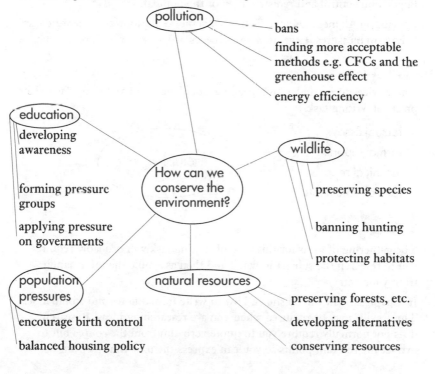

Having generated these ideas, you would need to decide on the organisation and development of the essay. You may decide that the most effective way to deal with this subject is to organise your ideas into two groups.

threats	measures to adopt
Environmental pollution and loss of wildlife.	Laws and incentives which encourage industries to adopt a more responsible attitude to the environment.
Diminishing natural resources.	Effective preservation and conservation campaigns.
Population growth.	Education campaigns.

Your plan could be as follows:

Introduction Short historical overview of the growth of pollution and concern about its effects in recent years.

Development Importance of government action in passing laws and raising public awareness. Scientific developments to cut down on harmful emissions from heavy industry. Development of clean air campaigns. Population control and redistribution of the population.

Conclusion All methods are effective but some – education and scientific – are long-term measures. Legal framework necessary for everyone's protection.

Factual writing

The advice given under this heading could be applied to any factual or practical writing task.

factual essays
formal reports
technical reports
factual statements

factual writing

Helpful Hints

▶ The gathering of ideas for this type of writing task will probably require you to research the subject in detail and then assemble the information from your notes.

▶ In Chapter 8 you will be shown how to write formal notes and summarise. These skills may be required when you are researching ideas. Research does not normally require you to quote verbatim from the source but to extract the relevant points so you can express them in your own words.

▶ If it is possible, refer to several sources for the information you need. This will enable you to verify facts and/or consider a variety of opinions before you present your ideas.

▶ As the notes will be for your personal use, you don't need to adopt a formal layout but a careful use of headings and sub-headings will help you to organise the notes more effectively, and will make them easier to use for essays.

You have been shown several ways to approach idea gathering in this chapter, such as:

'spider' diagrams;

flow charts;

lists.

Choose the most appropriate method for your factual writing task.

Personal writing

There may be times when you decide to write for your own pleasure or to improve your skills. Obviously this book will provide you with a variety of writing situations but there may be other occasions when you want to write but are unable to find a suitable topic or theme.

Helpful Hints

It is usually easier to write from personal experience than create a purely imaginary scene or situation. Use events, characters or ideas from your life as starting points.

▶ Try describing the scene around you – the room you are sitting in, or the view from the window.

▶ If you visit a new place, try to sit and observe the scene for a few minutes. Jot down your impressions so you can develop them later. Many professional writers carry a small note book around with them to record ideas that they can incorporate into their books – follow their example.

▶ 'Brainstorm' a topic (e.g. a news item), and jot down all the ideas you associate with it. Select those that stimulate your imagination or memory.

▶ Use words as 'triggers'. This is especially successful for descriptive writing.

Choose a word, 'brainstorm' it and refer to a dictionary and thesaurus to add to your ideas.

e.g.

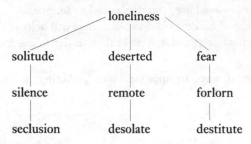

Think about the images that these words conjure up for you. You could describe:

a remote, deserted abandoned house;

a lonely old man or woman abandoned by family and friends;

a remote, peaceful, secluded place where you can sit and think in solitude.

By letting your imagination range over the ideas, you should soon find one that stimulates you to write.

▶ Use your reading as a stimulus. You may like to take a scene from a book and try to write about it from a different viewpoint.

▶ Pictures can also provide suitable inspiration, not only for descriptive writing but also as a starting point for a story.

Final thoughts

This chapter has provided you with a great deal of information about the initial stages of writing – gathering and organising ideas.

You need to plan

before starting most formal writing tasks,

if you are faced with a difficult or unfamiliar informal writing situation, *or*

if there are several points to be included.

We have suggested different planning approaches according to the task, but you can choose the approach that you find most helpful and effective.

- Careful planning will help you to write more confidently and effectively.
- Good planning is evident to the trained eye.
- A well-planned piece of formal writing usually has an introduction, a development and a conclusion.

Now that you have worked through Section 1 you have considered all the writing skills. You will probably feel you need to return to certain chapters or parts of a chapter again as you carry out the writing tasks in Section 2. Skills which aren't utilised lose their freshness so put your writing skills into practice and write as much as possible.

7

8
Summary Skills

> v.t. **summarise, -ize** to present in summary or briefly –
>
> adj. **summary** condensed: brief –
>
> n. an abridgement

When we summarise speech or writing, we express the main points briefly in our own words.

An everyday skill

Summarising is a practical, everyday skill.

At an interview for a job you will summarise the main aspects of your past experience, skills, ambitions, etc. in order to answer the interviewer's questions briefly yet thoroughly.

If you are asked about a television programme you have seen or a newspaper article you have read, you will pick out the main points and outline these briefly – this is the skill of summarising.

SUNDAY FEBRUARY 1st

Snowed all day – went for a walk in the park.
Photo evening with Ben and Phil.

MONDAY FEBRUARY 2nd

More snow overnight – walked to work. Not many
people in. Telephone didn't stop – all complaints.

TUESDAY FEBRUARY 3rd

I took Paul and Clive to Feckenham for the concert.
Paul played well – Clive mimed.

THE FOURTH PROTOCOL
is the story of a plan,
dangerous beyond belief, to change the face of British society for ever.

Plan Aurora, hatched in a remote dacha in the forest outside Moscow, and initiated with relentless brilliance and skill, is a plan that in its madness – and spine-chilling ingenuity – breaches the ultra-secret Fourth Protocol and turns the fears that shaped it into a living nightmare.

A crack Soviet agent, placed under cover in a quiet English country town, begins to assemble a jigsaw of devastation. Working blind against the most urgent of deadlines, and against treachery and lethal power games in his own organisation, MI5 investigator John Preston leads an operation to prevent the act of murderous devastation aimed at tumbling Britain into revolution.

NANNY REQUIRED

8.30 – 5.00 daily.

Term time only.

Non smoker. Driver.

Tel. 0789 564381

The writer of the diary entries has included each day's highlights; a brief outline of the story is given on the back cover of the paperback book; and only essential information is included in the job advertisement.

** Write a short paragraph to outline the story of a book you have recently read or a television programme you have seen.

We practise summary skills at home, at work and for study purposes in these situations:

INFORMAL LETTERS

We include any points of interest to our reader.

FORMAL LETTERS

For our letters to be effective, we select the relevant points and express them succinctly.

CVs

We briefly include all the necessary information about ourselves.

MEMORANDA

A memo should be concise and exact.

ESSAYS

We select information which will most aptly describe or support the title and record this concisely.

MINUTES

The main points of discussions are recorded exactly and concisely in an agreed format.

REPORTS

The main points are presented directly, clearly and in an orderly arrangement.

MESSAGES

In both informal and formal messages only the main points are included.

INSTRUCTIONS

Clear, brief directions are given, often in numbered points.

EXAMINATIONS

We produce essential information in enough detail to answer the question.

COMPREHENSION QUESTIONS

In English and in other subjects we have to summarise what we have read in order to answer specific questions. Often we are asked to express our answers in a given number of words.

STATEMENTS

e.g. A statement to support a job application will concisely summarise your qualifications and experience which make you suitable for the job.

What are the summary skills?

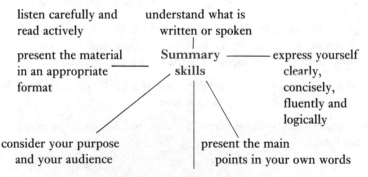

listen carefully and read actively

understand what is written or spoken

present the material in an appropriate format

Summary skills

express yourself clearly, concisely, fluently and logically

consider your purpose and your audience

present the main points in your own words

understand the vocabulary used and use exact, appropriate vocabulary yourself

Listening

Listening to someone speak and passing on the essence of what the speaker has said is something we all do quite naturally in informal situations. We may pass on this information verbally, or write a message or note. Sometimes it will be necessary to convey all the main points; at other times passing on selected information – a selective summary – is what is required.

Formal listening tasks require more thought and concentration. We may be:

▸ making notes of a lecture for our own use or for another person;

▸ noting down information to write up the minutes of a meeting;

▸ noting down information to write a report;

▸ listening to instructions in order to carry out a task or procedure.

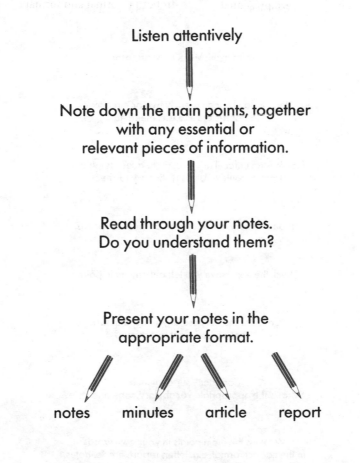

Listen attentively

Note down the main points, together with any essential or relevant pieces of information.

Read through your notes. Do you understand them?

Present your notes in the appropriate format.

notes   minutes   article   report

More advice is given about formal note taking later in this chapter.

When we listen, we only have the opportunity to listen to information once so it is important to concentrate as it is all too easy to miss important points. Being an active listener is a skill that many people need to practise. We have all probably had the experience of being introduced to a person and immediately forgetting his or her name, or suddenly realising we have just missed a vital part of a talk we were supposed to be following.

Cultivate the listening habit.

Reading

When you have a passage of writing that you need to summarise,

Read it through to gain a general impression.

Ask yourself: What is its purpose?

Read it slowly and carefully two or three times to appreciate its exact meaning.

If there is an unfamiliar word, try to guess its meaning from its context. Use a dictionary to check.

From memory, make a list of all the main points.

Check the text. Have you left out any main points?

Consider the purpose of your writing task. What do you want to achieve?

Consider your audience. What is the appropriate vocabulary, tone and style?

Write up the main points in your own words in the correct format, e.g. letter, report, article, notes.

Proof-read your writing. Check:

the spelling, punctuation and grammar;

the vocabulary: is it appropriate?

it reads smoothly as a piece of writing.

Have you expressed the essential ideas of the original in a brief, clear manner?

Helpful Hints

▶ Always consider the task carefully before you begin. Do you need to make a complete summary including all the main points, or do you need to make a selective summary?

▶ It is usually better to put the passage to one side when you are trying to recall the main points. If you follow the passage through, trying to summarise it as you go, you may find yourself using the author's words. However, when faced with a complicated passage, it may be necessary to go through it point by point, summarising each in turn.

▶ You do not need to include supporting details, examples or illustrations, only the main points.

▶ It is not necessary to present the information in your summarised version in the same order as it appears in the original text, but it is important to present information in a logical order. Sometimes it is helpful to alter the order when you want to link ideas together to create a fluent piece of writing.

▶ Don't alter the sense of a passage you have read or listened to when you summarise it.

▶ Make certain you have not added opinions or knowledge of your own even if they seem relevant.

▶ You might be asked to incorporate several pieces of text into one overall summary. For example, you might have to read several letters and summarise the main points from all of them, or read several sources and present the main arguments in an essay, report or article.

You can tackle this task in a similar way by summarising each individually and then including all the essential points in your final piece of writing. Take care not to present the same piece of information twice: the same point may occur in more than one source. You may need to make a plan before you write the final version as it will be important to consider the order in which you present the information.

Your summarised version should be clear, straightforward and read naturally.

** Read this passage about 'Champagne Flights'. The writer uses a great many words to give a few simple facts because he is trying to persuade as well as inform. Write a paragraph summarising the main points. Check your version with the answer section. Although your answer will be slightly different, you should have included the same main points and omitted the details.

Champagne Flights

CHAMPAGNE FLIGHTS INTERNATIONAL has been formed to offer you what is often thought of by many as the ultimate adventure – <u>a flight in a Hot Air Balloon</u>.

The awe-inspiring sight of a Balloon meandering over the open countryside is breathtakingly beautiful; just imagine being up there with them participating in that experience! The feeling is intensely exhilarating and the views so unreal that one has to submit to temptation and have a go!

We at CHAMPAGNE FLIGHTS believe that this, from start to finish, should be a memorable day for EVERYONE who takes up the challenge.

Flights are carried out all the year round, both in winter, when the conditions are cold and crisp, and in summer when light winds make the early mornings and late afternoons irresistible.

After an unforgettable flight, the Balloon eventually lands and the basket settles onto a grassy meadow. It's been an hour of perfect pleasure but the day would not be complete without that glass of 'bubbly'!

Finally, you are presented with your own 'First Flight' Certificate to commemorate the occasion and are then transported back to the launch site.

Many Champagne Flights are given as Birthday or Anniversary presents, with numerous companies using them as hospitality flights. But by far the greatest majority of flights are made by those people like you or I who have dreamt for so long of taking one. So why not make fantasy a reality and book one yourself, now, and don't forget your camera!

Note taking

Notes help to jog our memories as it is impossible to remember everything we hear or read.

Formal notes

These should be brief, clear, provide information at a glance and be suitable for the intended purpose and audience.

Notes which you use for personal study purposes will need to be clear and concise; they should make sense to you, not only when you write them but when you refer to them at a later date. You may well use abbreviations that are only meaningful to you.

Notes written for another person (e.g. notes of a technical article for your boss to use) must be sufficiently clear to make sense to your audience; avoid personal abbreviations.

Helpful Hints

▶ Listen or read carefully and select the main points from the text.
▶ Record your notes carefully and concisely. There is no need to write in sentences but use sufficient words to make meaning clear.
▶ Use meaningful headings: main headings and sub headings.
▶ Start each new point on a new line.
▶ Number points if a logical order is apparent.
▶ Use capital letters or underline in colour to draw attention to headings or key words/phrases.
▶ Use the space you have in an imaginative way – this can help you remember the information.
▶ Use standard abbreviations but, for study purposes, devise and use your own abbreviations as well.

** Consider in which ways the two sets of notes overleaf fail to follow our advice for note taking.

HENRY VIII

1491–1547 (Windsor)

Ref. of Eng.

2nd son of Henry VII (married x6)

Catherine of Aragon (b's widow) 1509 → divorce

Anne Boleyn → Eliz. I

Jane Seymour → Ed. VI (died)

Handsome

International Dialling

Country Code

Int Code

010 1st

A. Town

No.

DD cheaper

Cheap 8–8 wkend - time diff

When you look at notes, you should be able to:

understand them immediately;

select specific information by using the headings.

** Study the notes below and then use them to write a brief article entitled 'Accommodation for Walkers'.

WALKING IN BRITAIN

1 Advice

Wear strong footwear

Take waterproof jacket and trousers

Ordnance survey map essential

Respect Country Code

Country Code

Respect life/work of countryside

Guard against fire risk

Fasten gates

Keep dogs under control

Use public paths

Use gates/stiles

Take litter home

Don't contaminate water

Protect wildlife/plants/trees

2 Accommodation

a Youth Hostels

Operated by YHA

Membership necessary

Details of hostels sent on joining

Charges reasonable

Bring sheet sleeping bag

b Camping Barns

Found in Peak District

Simple overnight shelter

Own equipment (sleeping/cooking) required

c Camping Sites

Details of official sites – local tourist offices

Unofficial camping – landowner's permission needed

Own equipment required

d Bed & Breakfast

Details – local tourist offices

Charges more than YHA but good value

3 Travel

a Bus – special 'go anywhere' tickets

b Train

c Car – transport from one centre to another

d Ferry – good service in Scotland – connect with bus and train – special 'Highland Travel Pass'

** Look at this list of standard abbreviations, then add others which you would find useful. The abbreviation section of a dictionary could help you.

&	and
a.s.a.p.	as soon as possible
∴	therefore
etc.	'etcetera' (and the rest)
e.g.	for example
N.B.	please note
i.e.	that is
" "	ditto marks (as above)
a.m.	morning
p.m.	afternoon
P.T.O.	please turn over
C₁₈ C₁₉	18th, 19th century
/	to separate items in a list of possibilities or alternatives
∵	because

Helpful Hints

▶ If you are noting down information from a book which you may want to refer to later for revision purposes, note down the book's title, author, publisher and the page numbers.

▶ When you use a book for research, you will save yourself time if you study the contents page and/or the index so that you can find the exact subject or aspect of the subject that you want to concentrate on. Within a chapter, it is often useful to scan through the headings so that you can identify the relevant sections before you start reading or making notes.

** Read the passage below. Produce a set of notes from it, under the title 'How Women Can Protect Themselves'. When you have completed them, compare them with the set of notes in the answer section.

Advice to Women

There are some sensible precautions that every woman should take to protect herself from attack whether she is at home, on foot or in the car.

Security at home is the most important consideration so adequate window and door locks and chains should be fitted and used.

Seek advice from your local police station, then consult a good DIY shop. If you move house, always change the door locks as strangers may have keys to your home. If you have any suspicions that a break-in has occurred, report it to the police at once.

When you answer the telephone, never give your name or number. List only your surname and initials in the telephone directory so that it is not obvious that you are a woman. Obscene or abusive calls can be very distressing but you should replace the receiver immediately and make no response. If the calls persist, inform the police and telephone operator and make certain you record the dates and times of such calls.

Special attention is required when you are walking alone. At night, use well-lit, main routes if at all possible and face oncoming traffic. Cross the street if you suspect you are being followed. If your suspicions are confirmed, work out the shortest route to a well-frequented place, and get there as quickly as possible.

As a motorist, it is important to plan your route using main roads whenever possible. Ensure your car is in good working order and has sufficient petrol for the journey. If possible, give details of your estimated time of arrival and route to someone at your destination so that if you fail to arrive the police can be alerted. Don't give lifts to hitch-hikers or stop to give any form of assistance unless you are sure it is a genuine emergency. After dark, park your car in well-lit streets or car parks and, when you return to your car, have your keys ready.

By being aware of the potential dangers in any situation and taking steps to minimise them, you will increase your sense of personal safety.

The art of making good notes depends upon your ability to select the most important points and record them in the clearest way possible.

Final thoughts

Summarising is an integral part of many formal writing tasks – a skill which you need to cultivate if you are to produce concise, relevant and effective pieces of writing. Don't think of it as being an academic exercise but a practical skill which you practise almost every day. **Think of the summarising skill as being the ability to produce the essential ideas of the original text simply and briefly in your own words.**

9
Letters

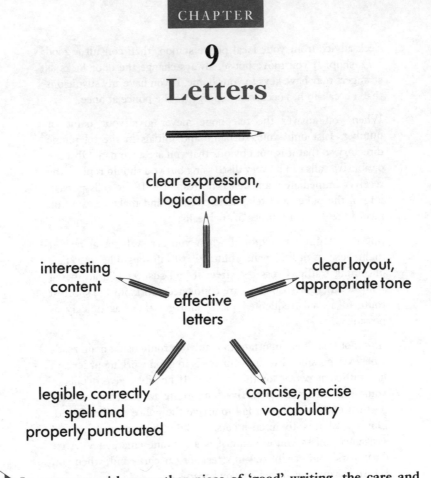

clear expression,
logical order

interesting
content

effective
letters

clear layout,
appropriate tone

legible, correctly
spelt and
properly punctuated

concise, precise
vocabulary

In common with any other piece of 'good' writing, the care and effort that has been spent on producing a letter will be obvious to the reader.

There may be occasions when you feel that your reader won't mind if your letter is not perfect but if you always try to produce a well-written letter, you should find your letter-writing skills improve and you gain more satisfaction from the task.

Before you start to write any letter you should always ask yourself what type of letter you are writing. What is the situation? Who is your reader?

Types of letters

You should ask yourself:

What is the purpose of my letter?

Is this situation formal or informal?

How well do I know my reader?

How formal would my reader expect me to be?

Am I writing to one person or to several people?

Now decide whether your letter will be formal, semi-formal or informal. You must make this decision before you start to write as the **layout, style, vocabulary** and **tone** will be different according to which type of letter you are writing.

** Read the following extracts from letters and decide upon the formality of each. It will be helpful to check your ideas with the suggestions in the answer section before you continue with the chapter.

1 I'm sorry that Tom wasn't at school on Wednesday. Unfortunately he had a bad asthma attack on Tuesday evening which left him feeling very tired and wheezy.

2 Thank you for your order for Item No. 305691 which we received today.

3 It was an absolutely wonderful weekend which I shall never forget. I can't tell you how much it meant to me to see you all again.

4 I am sorry that you weren't at home when I called but I'll be working in your area again on Monday and, if it's convenient, could call in to see you at about 3.00 pm.

5 I was appalled by the comments made by Mr Smythe in last week's edition of *Opinions*.

6 My client regrets your decision to proceed with the matter but accepts the need to establish the exact position of the boundary.

7 As you are aware, our group always has a yearly get-together: this year we have decided to hold a cheese and wine party at the Chairman's house on Thursday 15 December. I hope that you'll be able to come and can promise a lively evening if past experience is anything to go by!

8 The car's going really well at the moment so I should arrive on time.

Informal letters

These are perhaps the easiest letters to write as we can be relaxed and use our everyday, colloquial vocabulary. However, we still need to make the letter interesting and convey our ideas clearly so certain guidelines should be followed.

Layout

By observing the accepted conventions for the layout of an informal letter, you will make it easier for your reader to follow your ideas.

72 Hay Street,
Dereham, ①
Sussex.
BR43 7BN
12 March 1992 ②

Dear Geoff, ③
　　I'm sure you'll be amazed to receive a letter from me after all this time but the other day I was sorting through some old papers and came across your address. I started to think about the holiday we all had in Spain and realised that after we came back, you moved and we gradually lost contact.

　　④ I hope that you have now settled down in Gosport and you're enjoying your new job. I'm sure it is very different to GKL. Bob Walker and I still talk about our famous training sessions. Do you remember them?

　　④ It would be good to meet you again and find out what you've been up to since you left Dereham. Both Carol and I would like you to come and stay one weekend, so if you have one free, give us a ring.

　　④ We look forward to hearing from you very soon.

　　　　Yours, ⑤
　　　　Derek

1 The writer puts his address at the top right-hand side of the letter.

2 This is followed by the date.

3 After the greeting there is a comma and the letter starts on the line directly below this comma.

4 Each new subject in the letter is shown by a new paragraph.

5 The letter ends with a closing phrase, followed by the writer's signature.

Helpful Hints

This is a handwritten letter so each line of the address has been indented. Each line of the address ends in a comma except for the county, which is followed by a full stop. The writer could have put a comma after the house number. Where appropriate the county can be abbreviated.

e.g. Wilts. (Wiltshire)

The date has been written in full.

i.e.   date   month   year
       | | |
       13   March   1992

Even in an informal letter this is preferable to writing the date in figures only.

The writer has chosen to close the letter with 'Yours'. As this is an informal letter to a friend, the decision about how to end the letter is entirely his own.

Decisions about closing phrases for informal letters can be difficult, as these letters to *The Times* demonstrate.

Sir,

I am concerned that there seems to be no way of ending a letter with a phrase which conveys the idea of 'in friendship'.

There is 'Love from'; there is 'Kind regards' but that seems rather formal; and 'Yours ever' implies all sorts of long-term commitments ... .

Sir,

Jan Pahl wants a letter ending to convey friendship not love or formality. How about 'Yours cordially' with which I have been ending letters for years?

The 'Yours' form is capable of all sorts of individual variations: 'Yours apologetically', 'Yours disgustedly', 'Yours in sackcloth and ashes', 'Yours delightedly' and I have used them all... .

Sir,

I have always thought of Evelyn Waugh's immortal phrase 'With love or what you will' as the ultimate end to all my correspondence... .

Helpful Hints

▶ It is not necessary to make a plan before writing informal letters but you may find it helpful to write a 'shopping list' of ideas as we suggested in Chapter 7. This enables you to make sure you include all the points you wish to make and helps you arrange your ideas in a logical order.

▶ Although you are not likely to write a first draft for an informal letter, you should read through the completed letter and correct any spelling or punctuation errors.

** You may like to practise your informal letter-writing skills and style by writing a letter to friends in which you thank them for a weekend you have just spent with them. Refer to the events of the weekend and suggest another visit.

Semi-formal letters

These letters cover a range of situations and relationships. They are usually personal letters, written about private rather than business or official matters, but they demand a greater degree of formality than we would normally use in an informal letter.

EXAMPLES:

a letter of sympathy to a friend or acquaintance

a letter to a neighbour who helped you during an emergency

a letter to a stranger who found and returned a lost wallet

a letter of congratulations from a manager to a junior colleague on his or her promotion

a letter to another member of a club or society

a letter to your child's teacher

▶ A handwritten semi-formal letter will have the same layout as a handwritten informal letter. (See page 116 for an example of this layout.)

▶ The writer will begin the letter by greeting the person by name.

EXAMPLES

Dear Simon,

Dear Mr Kennedy,

▶ Having begun the letter in this way, the writer would close with **Yours sincerely,**.

▶ If the reader is not familiar with the writer's name, the writer will usually print his or her name under the signature.

Ann Fanshaw

Ann Fanshaw

Appropriate tone

Semi-formal letters can be difficult to write when we are trying to convey our feelings as well as our ideas (for example, letters of condolence). We wish to sound sincere and genuine but often find it hard to choose the right words and set the appropriate tone.

By giving careful consideration to your reader, you should find it easier to adopt the right tone. Choose words that are suitable for the tone of the letter without using clichés or exaggerated or overwrought language.

EXAMPLES:

I was very sad to hear about … .

It was a great shock to learn of … .

She has always been a good friend and helped me on many occasions. I shall miss her.

Please do not hesitate to ask if, at any time in the future, you need help. I should like to think that I was able to offer you some of the support your father always gave me.

Formal letters

These are the business or official letters we write in our personal lives to:

> request information about a product;
>
> order goods;
>
> complain about a product or service;
>
> apply for a job;
>
> confirm arrangements.

At work we may also be involved in writing formal letters to:

> clients or customers;
>
> other organisations.

We may write formal letters as part of our social activities, for example as a secretary of a club or as a councillor.

▶ Formal letters require a good standard of English.

▶ We should use formal vocabulary which we may not have much practice in using.

▶ We know that our letters present people with their first impressions of us and we want them to be favourable.

▶ We may be representing our company or club so we want the letter to create the right image.

By knowing and observing the conventions for formal letters, and following the guidance given in this section, you should feel more confident about your ability.

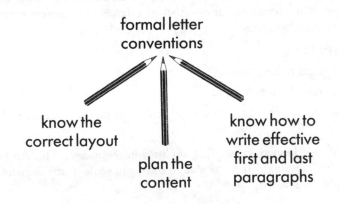

formal letter
conventions

know the
correct layout

plan the
content

know how to
write effective
first and last
paragraphs

Layout

This will vary according to whether the letter is handwritten or typed, or whether it should conform to an organisation's house style. In most handwritten letters the lines of the writer's address are indented and punctuated.

Example – handwritten formal letter:

> Flat 37,
>   Fletcher House,
>   Nechells,
>   Birmingham,
>   West Midlands.
>   B6 4 RF
>   27 September 1992
>
> Mrs H. Godfrey,
>   Production Manger,
>   W. R. Fewells Ltd.,
>   Castle Street,
>   Tamworth
>   Staffs.
>   ST32 9SD
>
> Dear Mrs Godfrey,
>   Thank you for your letter.....
>
>
>
>
>   Yours sincerely
>   Leslie Hopkins
>   Leslie Hopkins (Miss)

▶ The writer's address is at the top right-hand side of the page. This is followed by the date which must always be written in full in a formal letter.

▶ The name and address of the recipient starts on the line below the date. It is punctuated in the same way as the writer's address but each line starts close to the left hand margin (blocked not indented).

▶ The writer **does not** put his or her name above his or her address. It is printed after the signature. The name of the person who is being sent the letter **is** given before his or her address.

▶ In this letter the writer began

Dear Mrs Godfrey,

so ended with

Yours sincerely

When you use a person's name in the greeting you must end the letter 'Yours sincerely'. Check your spelling of 'sincerely'. (A good way of remembering it is to split the word into two: since/rely.)

▶ If the letter had started

Dear Sir,

or

Dear Madam,

the letter must end

Yours faithfully,

▶ Remember to use capital letters correctly in the greeting

e.g. Dear Sir,

and the close.

e.g. Yours faithfully,

The 's' of 'sincerely' and the 'f' of 'faithfully' start with a lower case letter.

Example – typed formal letter

Business Services
Unit 1
Roker Park
Bulverton
Herts
BV3 6TH

12 September 1992

The Manager
Dartford Fabrics
Kingfisher Precinct
Bulverton
Herts
BV3 17FG

Dear Sir,

I regret that our company is announcing an increase in its charges from 1 October 1992.

As you will be aware, we have maintained call-out charges at their present rates for the last two years. Unfortunately, the recent increases in fuel prices, coupled with higher labour costs mean that in order to continue to offer our guaranteed response service, we must pass on these increases to our customers. All call-out charges have been increased by 10%. However, materials and parts will remain at their present prices.

Please contact me if you require any further information about the proposed charges.

Yours faithfully,

J C Pettinger

J. C. Pettinger (Mrs)

(Customer Care Manager)

Note that both the addresses are **blocked not indented**.

In this instance the writer has chosen to put a comma after 'Dear Sir,' so a comma is used after 'Yours faithfully,'. Both of these commas could have been omitted.

A new paragraph in a blocked letter is not indented; a **double space** is left between paragraphs.

Variations in layout

Organisations often have a house style for the layout of their letters and may choose to centre their address or put the date on the left hand side of the letter.

Letters for publication in the letters section of a quality newspaper often follow a different convention.

The Editor
The Indicator
2 Fleet Road
London
EC1R 3ER

2 December 1992

Sir,

While I share Colin Bradshaw's concern about the destruction of the British countryside, I am not sure that refusing to pay taxes will have any beneficial effect; such action is very probably counter-productive.
    I suggest Mr Bradshaw reconsiders this rather foolhardy step and finds a more effective method of conveying his disquiet.

Donald Davies
The Mews
Fountain Walk
Chalfont St Giles
Bucks

Planning

You may find it helpful to refer to Chapter 7 where you were shown how to plan a formal letter and given advice on organising the content of your letter into paragraphs.

Careful planning is essential when writing a formal letter.

First and last paragraphs

These can be the most difficult parts of a letter to write.

The first paragraph of your letter usually outlines your reason for writing. Keep this paragraph simple and direct.

EXAMPLES:

Thank you for your letter of 4th December in which you expressed an interest in my ideas for a water cooled engine.

I wish to confirm the booking for two seats at the evening performance of 'Twelfth Night' on Saturday, 27th October.

On Saturday, 14th November I bought a BX mountain bike from your shop. Since then I have had to return it seven times to have various repairs carried out.

Further to our meeting on 2 December, I am sending you the details and costings for the Panasonic copiers.

We have now received the policy documents for your car insurance. We would therefore be grateful if you could send the premium of £123.00 as agreed during our telephone conversation on 3 May.

Avoid starting your letter with

I am writing to you about ... .

With reference to your letter of ... .

The last paragraph of a formal letter generally indicates to the reader the action you wish him or her to take. Be positive but polite.

EXAMPLES

I look forward to meeting you to discuss my ideas in more detail.

I would be grateful if you would confirm these arrangements.

We look forward to receiving your remittance within fourteen days.

I can assure you of this company's commitment to our customers and would appreciate your comments on the proposed changes.

If you require further copies of the poster, please contact me and I will arrange for them to be sent to you.

** Read the following passage and then write a suitable letter to Mr Collins, the Managing Director of Portman Engineering, Evensly Road, Luton.

On Friday 13th January you were visiting the firm and caught the sleeve of your new leather jacket on the overhanging wire perimeter fence of the firm's car park. This incident happened as you were trying to squeeze between your car and the fence in order to avoid a deep pot-hole full of water. The car park is in a poor state of repair with numerous holes, crumbling walls and broken fences. In spite of many complaints from employees, no action has been taken.

Advice about writing formal letters

Use exact, direct words in your formal letters. Avoid 'officialese' or 'business English' – pompous or convoluted language.

e.g.

> The Council acknowledges receipt of your letter re. membership fees. Although we may concur with the sentiments you utter, we are unable to make a response until after the meeting arranged for 15 June. If you would care to attend the aforesaid meeting and direct our attention once more to the matter, we may be able to arrive at a mutually agreeable settlement.

A simpler and more direct way to express this would be:

> The Council thanks you for your letter about membership fees. Although we are in sympathy with your views, we are unable to comment until after the meeting on 15 June. If you could attend this meeting to discuss the matter with us, we may be able to reach a compromise.

Do not use:

jargon;

colloquial English;

slang;

clichés

in formal letters.

Be concise. Be disciplined about the number of words you use. Your reader will not wish to study a long, wordy letter that fails to make its purpose clear.

Proof-read and edit your first draft carefully. Remember to check its:

spelling;

punctuation;

content;

tone.

Proof-read your final copy before sending it.

Chapter 10 gives advice about job application letters and Chapter 11 provides guidance on standard business letters.

Final thoughts

As this chapter contains a considerable amount of advice and guidance, you may need to refer to it from time to time to check that you are clear about all the points it has covered.

Look critically at letters you receive.

Are they well-written?

Do they follow the accepted conventions?

Do they make their points clearly and concisely?

It may be helpful to collect 'good' phrases and sentences from other people's letters and then use them in your own.

** Consider the following letter and assess its strengths and weaknesses. You will find our comments in the **Answers**.

West Mercia Electricity
Mercia Way
Coventry CV5 8HU

Mr F. Henderson   13 December 1992
34 Field Gardens
Allesley   Our Ref: 43/EF/1
Coventry CV12 6TY

Dear Mr Henderson,

In reply to your letter dated 21 November 1992 of which I regret you have found reason to complain about our service.

In view of the time elapsed and no response has been received from your letter regarding further work which you may require from West Mercia Electricity. In the interest of good customer relations, I have now cancelled the charge for this service.

Please accept my apologies for the inconvenience caused through this matter, if we can be of any further assistance, please do not hesitate to contact me.

Yours faithfully,

V. Southern

Customer Enquiries Department

10
Applying for a job

For many people the most crucial test of their writing is when they apply for a job. The majority of job applications involve:

   writing letters;

   completing job application forms;

   producing curriculum vitae.

As these are the first impressions the prospective employer receives of the applicant, it is essential that they are effective.

What makes an effective written application?

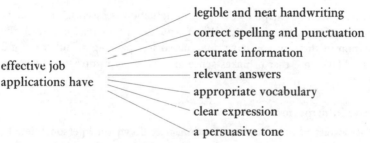

effective job applications have
- legible and neat handwriting
- correct spelling and punctuation
- accurate information
- relevant answers
- appropriate vocabulary
- clear expression
- a persuasive tone

Legible and neat handwriting

Perhaps the most obvious point about any written application is that it should be easy to read. Letters and application forms may be handwritten or typed, but CVs should always be typed.

The overall appearance of any job application is very important. Whether handwritten or typed, it should not contain any mistakes or words crossed through.

In order to produce a perfect final copy you will have to prepare a first draft, and carefully proof-read and edit it. It's a good idea to show your first draft to friends or family for their comments before you write it up.

Your application will be viewed more favourably if your handwriting and layout are clear and careful. When an employer receives numerous applications he or she could initially decide to reject

Section 2

10

those which are untidy, difficult to read and poorly presented.

Correct spelling and punctuation

You must proof-read your first draft to check the spelling of any words you are uncertain about. You may have difficulty with company and place names which often appear to have illogical spellings. You could check them by referring to any letters or information you have received from the company, using a gazeteer for place names, or referring to a telephone or business directory.

A list of relevant 'employment' words can be useful for quick reference.

EXAMPLES:

refer<u>e</u>nce

exper<u>ie</u>nce

exper<u>tise</u>

respons<u>ibities</u>

person<u>nel</u>

As you have seen in Chapter 4, correct punctuation is essential in order to convey your message correctly. When you are proof-reading, read the information in the way you have punctuated it – pausing at full stops and commas. Make sure that it makes sense and, where appropriate, is written in sentences.

Accurate information

Before you start to write your application, note down your personal details, including qualifications gained and employment history to date.

Check these dates and other details are correct and if possible find the relevant certificates, contracts or documents.

When you have completed your application, check that the details you have given are correct – it is easy to give the wrong date or forget to include important facts about yourself. (See also the section **Preparation** on page 132.)

Relevant answers

Make certain that the answers or information you give are relevant to your application.

Be concise – employers do not have time to read long, rambling accounts of your personal life!

Ensure that the points you make are worthwhile and pertinant.

Appropriate vocabulary

Job applications require a formal tone even if you are applying for promotion within your own organisation and know the person who will deal with your application.

In this chapter we have used the phrase 'applying for a job', but in an application letter you should use more formal vocabulary.

EXAMPLES:

I wish to apply for the position of ... .

I wish to be considered for the post of ... .

Listed below are other phrases which you might find useful when applying for a job.

I am responsible for ... .

My present duties include ... .

I would like to be involved in ... .

Although I have no formal qualifications ... .

I am familiar with many aspects of ... .

use my initiative/expertise/skills/experience ... .

have experience in ... .

sending you my CV which outlines my ... .

make a positive contribution to ... .

look forward to meeting you to discuss ... .

I can assure you of my commitment to ... .

I would be grateful if you could ... .

I am available for interview ... .

Please do not hesitate to contact me if you require any further information concerning ... .

Clear expression

If you have carried out adequate preparation, you should find that you can express your ideas clearly and coherently. The most difficult, but also most important, parts of any application are:

saying why you would like to be considered for this job;

stating why you would be the most suitable applicant.

We give you help with these two points later in this chapter.

A first draft allows you to try out different ways of expressing yourself and to select the most effective sentences. It is unlikely that you will be completely satisfied with your first draft. Spend time developing your ideas until you are happy with how they are expressed.

A persuasive tone

Your job application 'sells' you to a potential employer. Be positive and enthusiastic; point out how your achievements, qualities and experience make you a suitable person for the position. Careful preparation will ensure that you identify your own 'selling points' and present them in a persuasive way.

Preparation

▶ Gather information about yourself
▶ Analyse the job
▶ Consider your presentation

Gather information about yourself

Factual

List all the factual information about yourself that you need to include in a job application. Include:

> names of schools and colleges you have attended;
>
> details of any qualifications (dates and grades) you have achieved;
>
> names and addresses of people who are willing to provide a reference for you.

It is useful to keep this information in a file so that it is accessible. Don't forget to update it from time to time!

Personal attributes

These are the factors that you will need to consider when 'selling' yourself to an employer. Be objective about your own

> strengths and weaknesses,
>
> experience,
>
> achievements, and
>
> abilities.

To sell yourself you must be positive about your strengths, but be honest about your weaknesses and try to minimise their effects.

LIST YOUR STRENGTHS – those aspects of your character or behaviour which you would admire in others or think may be advantageous to the company.

Are you
- trustworthy?
- punctual?
- keen to succeed?

Try to relate these strengths to situations in your working life. You may be able to refer to these in your application or during your interview.

CONSIDER YOUR WEAKNESSES – those aspects that may make you less attractive to an employer. Although you won't mention weaknesses as such in an application, you may be asked to consider them at interview, so try to turn them into positive features.

For example, you may have had a gap in your employment when you were bringing up children. Consider the benefits that this gave you and how you could present this in a favourable and positive way to an employer – it may have allowed you to gain more qualifications, given you greater maturity, better organisational skills or increased your motivation to succeed.

LIST YOUR WORK EXPERIENCE – try to recall your exact duties and responsibilities as this helps you to provide relevant and precise details in your application. Your relevant experience does not always have to be work-related. Consider your social activities and interests – have these provided any worthwhile experience? Once again you will need to list the relevant aspects precisely.

For example, an applicant for a position as a travel courier might list the following interests and activities.

Youth club leader – organised activity and outward bound holidays in Britain and Europe for parties of young people – sole responsibility for travel arrangements.

First aider – held certificate for last three years – in attendance as first aider at various sports and charity meetings.

Spent six months in Spain in 1985 – can speak Spanish, understand Spanish way of life and know something about Spanish culture.

NOTE DOWN YOUR ACHIEVEMENTS, both personal and work related. Think about what you have achieved, how you achieved it and how this could be relevant to your application.

10

For example, to demonstrate your team spirit, you might mention that you have been selected to be a member of your county's hockey team, demonstrating skill, perseverance, commitment and ability to perform as part of a team. This shows a high level of commitment to an organisation and determination to improve your performance.

Think about what your abilities are.

DIY?

organising yourself
and others? ————————————————— Are you good at

communicating?

Define why you are good at each of these, what you like about them and consider how this may help you in a work situation – the skills and knowledge you use in these areas may be transferable. Find examples of occasions or situations where your abilities have contributed to a successful outcome.

For example, practical skills gained through DIY may improve your dexterity in other operations and enhance your ability to solve problems. You may have been able to learn new work-related skills more quickly because of your DIY activities.

When you have considered all these aspects of your personal attributes, you will:

> have a useful profile of yourself,
>
> be able to provide precise details about yourself,
>
> be able to match your experience and qualities to a job more accurately,
>
> be able to sell yourself more effectively because you will be more aware of your abilities and strengths, and
>
> be able to provide actual examples to illustrate the contribution you could make to an organisation.

Analyse the job

If you are responding to an advertisement for a job vacancy, study it carefully. Underline or list the employer's requirements.

BOLTON INSURANCE

With 20 offices in the Northern region we are the largest regional insurance company. Our excellent reputation for a quality customer service has enabled us to expand rapidly which is why we are now actively seeking to increase our staff.

CLAIMS CLERK

You will be dealing with a variety of claims and the attendant paperwork. This position calls for <u>an excellent telephone manner</u> as you will be required to <u>offer customers a prompt, efficient service</u>. You will also need to <u>possess good writing skills</u>, as part of your responsibilities will involve you in <u>preparing reports and writing letters</u>. Preference will be given to <u>experienced</u> claims clerks as you <u>must be able to work with little supervision</u>.

Now consider what else the employer might be looking for in an applicant. List these additional points.

For example, in the job advertised above, it might be advantageous for the applicant to be able to type and have good organisational skills.

Having considered the requirements of the job, you must now look back at the information you have gathered about yourself and see how far you match the requirements. This will not only help you to decide whether you have sufficient experience or qualifications to apply for the position, it will also enable you to sell yourself successfully in your application.

CLAIMS CLERK

Requirements	My experience and abilities
an excellent telephone manner	obtained City & Guilds Communication Skills Level 3 and attended 5-day course on telephone skills in 1989
offer customers prompt, efficient service	promoted in last company because my department reached its efficiency targets
good writing skills	English GCSE and experience of writing reports and letters in previous jobs

10

prefer experienced claims clerk	3 years at Hill Insurance Services, Bexhill – started as general clerk promoted to claims clerk with similar duties – handled 250 claims in 1991
work with little supervision	my supervisor has been away on sick leave for 3 months – presently supervising 4 junior clerks – have handled several large claims during this time
good keyboard skills	RSA Typing Stage 3
organisational skills	reorganised filing system and data bank at Hill Insurance Services

Consider your presentation

Often you will not be given a choice as to how you present your application. Company policy will dictate whether you send a CV or complete an application form. However, if you send a speculative application, you need to decide whether to include a full CV with your letter or merely provide a brief résumé. Brief details are more likely to be read and kept on file. (In the section on curriculum vitae on page 137 you will be shown both formats.)

If you are required to submit an application form, it is sometimes desirable to send an accompanying letter which emphasises your suitability and enthusiasm for the position. (See pages 143-5)

Job application forms

Forms obviously vary according to the organisation and their recruitment policy, but generally they cover these aspects:

    personal details,
    details of education and training,
    employment history,
    health,
    interests and leisure activities.

Many application forms have a section in which you are asked to give your reasons for applying for the position. If this is not on the form, refer to your reasons and suitability in your accompanying letter. Use the information you collected when you 'matched' yourself to the job to point out your suitability, and refer to those aspects of the job that interest you.

▶ Photocopy the application form and use the copy to practise. Perhaps someone could check this draft for you before you copy the information on to the original.

▶ Read through the entire form before you start. This will ensure you include the correct details in each section and prevent repetition.

▶ Read and follow any instructions you are given for completing the form.

▶ Unless you are asked to complete certain sections of the form in block capitals, write your answers in lower case letters – you are less likely to make spelling mistakes.

▶ Remember to respond in positive ways to the questions and present yourself in a favourable way.

Curriculum vitae

This may also be referred to as a CV or Career History. You will be presenting information similar to that which an employer would require in an application form, but you will have more control over which aspects of your career you emphasise and the order you present the information. In effect, you can present a more individual, distinct and personalised picture of yourself which, hopefully, will make a better impression on a potential employer.

Headings

The information you present about yourself will be divided up into several sections. It is advisable to head these to help the reader find the relevant details easily and quickly. Possible headings include:

Personal details

Education and training

Qualifications

Employment (experience and achievements)

Additional information

All CVs start by providing personal details but thereafter you can present the information in whatever order you feel most clearly reflects your strengths. Don't provide too much detail under each heading but emphasise the aspects of your life which you feel are most important and 'sell' you most effectively to a potential employer.

EXAMPLES:

A school or college leaver may present details about his or her education first. Brief details of any casual employment that support the application would be shown later.

Someone with considerable work experience but who had achieved little success at school may be advised to present employment details first, showing achievements in this area. He or she could then briefly outline any qualifications and training, and list schools attended.

Example of a curriculum vitae

CURRICULUM VITAE

Name | Joan Clarke

Address | 120 Haulton Road
Haulton
Durham DH15 7BE

Tel. no. | 0561 321674

Date of birth | 21 April 1967

Marital status | Single | Nationality | English

Employment experience and achievements
February 1990 – present
Foulkes Estate Agents, Gisborough
Position: **Senior Negotiator**
Whilst this position involves me in property sales, I am also responsible for the day-to-day running of the office. As the office opened in 1990, part of my initial responsibilities included establishing working practices and procedures. The office achieved its 1990 sales targets within the first six months of opening.

February 1986 – February 1990
William Deakman Estate Agents, Haulton; Gisborough and
Highley
Position: **Sales Negotiator**
I was involved in all aspects of estate agency from initial
valuation through to sale completion. In 1989 I achieved the
highest sales figures within the company and won the
company's 'Negotiator of the Year' award.

June 1985 – February 1986
Thetfords Auctioneers, Valuers and Estate Agents, Durham
Position: Assistant to Senior Partner
My duties involved me in the agricultural side of the firm and
my responsibilities included assisting with rent reviews,
boundary disputes, arbitrations, farm valuations and auctions.

Education and Training
1979 – 1984 Haulton High School, Haulton, Durham.
1984 – 1985 Durham College of Further Education
O levels in English, Mathematics, Physics, History and
Geography.

In-house training has included courses on establishing a data-
base, sales promotion techniques, customer relations and a new
managers' course.

Additional information

Interests
Swimming: I am a member of Durham Swimming Club and
have represented Durham in various swimming events.
Walking: I recently completed a sponsored Pennine Way walk
for MENCAP.
Reading
Cooking

I hold a current driving licence with no endorsements.
Health   No health problems

Referees
Mr C. Middleway   Mr C. Foulkes
Williams, Stanley and Davit Managing Director
28 Imperial Square   Foulkes Estate Agents
Durham   Theobury House
DH1 4WE   Gisborough DH19 6TH

A résumé

This provides brief details of your career. You may wish to send it with a speculative letter to a company. If the company is interested in you, you may be asked to send a more detailed CV.

CAREER RESUME

Name Roger Deakins

Address 24 School Road, Stratford, Warwickshire. CV35 3ER

Tel. 0789 6784

Date of birth 4 August 1950

Marital status Married

Education and Qualifications
'O' level passes in English, maths, physics and technical drawing.

City & Guilds Telecoms	Foundation, A, B & C years Radio Communication, Basic Radar, Microwave Techniques

Work Experience

1975 to present	Birmingham International Airport Radio technician – maintenance of communication equipment, microwave links and CCTV
1967 – 1975	Midlands Electricity Board – apprentice in Telephone/Telemetry Dept – PBX and telemetry maintenance in West Midlands area

---

Helpful Hints

▶ A résumé or CV should always be typed on one side of the page only. If you have photocopies made, make sure they are as clear as the original.

▶ Keep the information within the CV concise – aim for a maximum of two pages of A4.

▶ In a full CV include details of your employment:

your achievements;

your duties and responsibilities.

▶ You will probably be using your CV to apply for a number of jobs – it is unlikely that you will 'tailor' it for each application, nor will an employer expect you to do so. You should send a letter with the CV pointing out the relevance of your qualifications and achievements. See pages 143–5 for advice about such letters.

Job application letters

In this section we shall consider the variety of letters that you may need to write when applying for a job.

▶ Letters requesting an application form

▶ Letters to accompany an application for an advertised vacancy

▶ Speculative letters

▶ Letters to confirm an interview

▶ Letters to accept a job offer

The letters you write in connection with applying for a job should always follow the layout and style of a formal letter. Refer to Chapter 9 for detailed advice about formal letters.

Plan your letter and write a first draft. Proof-read your final copy before you send it.

142 Manor Road
Southend-on-Sea,
Essex
EX34 6PT
14 September 1992

Mr G Brady,
Personnel Manager,
ETS Ltd,
Long Lane,
Dagenham,
Essex. EX12 5RT

Dear Mr Brady

    I am interested in the vacancy for a fitter which was advertised in the 'Dagenham News' on 13th September. I would be grateful if you could send me an application form and further details of this position.

    Yours sincerely,

Trevor Richards

Trevor Richards

The writer refers to the advertisement, the position, and requests an application form. No other information is given. Keep such letters brief – do not include any personal details as your potential employer won't be interested in them at this stage.

Letters to accompany an application

These letters require careful preparation as they emphasise your suitability for the position. Look back to the section about preparation on page 132. In that section you identified your personal attributes and were given guidance on matching them to the requirements of a job. The points that are identified during this process form the major part of the accompanying letter.

DUFFIELD HOSPITAL

REQUIRES A

SOUS CHEF

An exciting opportunity has arisen at this prestigious private hospital.

You will need

★ City & Guilds 706/1-2 (Additional qualifications are desirable)

★ Good Private Hospital/Hotel Restaurant Experience

★ Ability to Implement New Costings Structure

★ Previous Supervisory Experience

16 Wealden Avenue
Wolverhampton
West Midlands
B56 FG3
20th December
1992

Mr K Singh
Hospital Services Manager
Duffield Hospital
Dudley B12 7YM

Dear Mr Singh

I wish to apply for the position of sous chef
which was advertised in the 'Wolverhampton
Gazette' on 15th December 1992.

As you will see from my C.V., I not only have
City and Guilds 706/1-2 but also 706/3 and
N.E.B.S.M. qualifications and have had several
years' experience in hotel and private hospital
catering. In my present position my
responsibilities include the supervision of four
members of staff. I recently attended a
training course on cost control and feel
confident that I could implement your new
costings structure.

I understand that you are interested in
developing a vegetarian menu. My present
company recently asked me to include several
vegetarian dishes on our lunch menu. Since then
there has been a 15% increase in the use of the
restaurant at lunch times. I have enjoyed the
challenge of creating interesting vegetarian
dishes and am keen to extend my experience.

I am confident that my qualifications and
experience could make a positive contribution to
your hospital service and look forward to
meeting you to discuss the position further.

Yours sincerely,

Jackie Colman

Jackie Colman (Ms)

Note that:

the writer refers to the position and advertisement;

she indicates that she has sent a CV with the letter;

she has identified the requirements of the job and shown how she matches them;

the letter ends on a positive note.

The sample letter given opposite is organised into four paragraphs.

Paragraph 1: the reason for writing.

Paragraphs 2 and 3: the main body of the letter, emphasising the suitability of the applicant.

Paragraph 4: the closing statement.

Speculative letters

These are letters which are written to employers on the off chance that they may be recruiting. They are not written in response to an advertisement. Such an approach will only be successful if:

you have carried out the necessary research;

you write a letter that is sufficiently interesting and persuasive to capture the employers' attention.

Preparation and research

▶ Find out which companies or organisations are involved in your type of work. You can find this information in the reference section of a local library or by looking at local business directories, newspapers, trade magazines, etc.

▶ Research the organisation – find out exactly which products it makes or which services it offers.

▶ Consider the contribution you could make to the company. (Refer to your list of personal attributes to see how your experience, abilities or achievements may be of interest.)

▶ Find out a contact name at the company. Your letter is more likely to be read if it is addressed to a named person.

The letter

Your plan for the letter could follow the following arrangement.

Paragraph 1: The reason for your letter – refer to the possibility of a job vacancy.

Paragraph 2: Brief details outlining the contribution you could make to the company (refer to your personal attributes).

Paragraph 3: Conclusion – refer to the CV or résumé which you are sending with the letter.

Letters of confirmation and acceptance

These days you will probably confirm your attendance at an interview with a telephone call, but occasionally you may need to write a letter. Such letters should be brief, courteous and positive.

---

6 Witherford Way
Petersfield
Hants SH46 8KL
November 23rd 1992

Ms P Danby
James Gough & Sons
Bearwood House
The Square
Petersfield
Hants SH45 3VB

Dear Ms Danby

Thank you for your letter of 22nd November. I shall be pleased to attend the interview on Wednesday 30th November at 10.00 pm.

I look forward to meeting you.

Yours sincerely,

Glenys Streeter

Glenys Streeter (Miss)

Similarly, in your letter confirming your acceptance of a job you will agree to the arrangements and express your eagerness to start work!

11
Business Writing

We are probably more aware of shortcomings in our writing skills when we are at work than when we are writing for our own personal use. Unfortunately, the more we worry the more likely we are to make mistakes.

As well as being confident about the many skills that make up writing, we also need to feel we are capable of carrying out the specific writing tasks that our particular job demands. Most jobs have a set of routine writing tasks associated with them. By acquiring the knowledge needed to fulfil these activities we gradually become proficient at our particular jobs: only when we change jobs or the nature of our jobs alters in some way do we need to acquire the techniques of other writing tasks.

In Chapter 8 we looked at summary skills which form the basis of the formal writing activities we carry out at work; in Chapter 9 we looked specifically at letter writing. In this chapter we will consider

messages,

memorandums,

notices,

instructions,

job descriptions,

statements and reports,

standard letters,

meetings (agendas and minutes).

Messages

We are all accustomed to writing messages for our family and friends in which we briefly note down the main points. In the same way, the messages we write at work concisely outline the main points but are usually recorded in more formal language.

The formality of the language depends upon our audience. We need to consider what our audience expects from us. e.g. If one of your colleagues is also a close friend, you may leave this message for him.

Fraser

Have borrowed your maintenance manual for a meeting. Give it to you later.

Cheers

Hugh

The informal language and layout reflect the writer's relationship with the reader – the style is appropriate to their friendship. However, the same message would be unsuitable for a colleague with whom you had only a working relationship.

Messages often form a record of the transaction of business within a company and so are regarded as formal documents. Companies frequently use standard message pads.

EXAMPLES:

MESSAGE

DATE *October 17th 1992*

TIME *3.30 p.m.*

TO *Rebecca Armstrong*

Your leaflets have been completed are are ready for collection from room B219

SIGNATURE *B. Hemmings*

WHILE YOU WERE OUT

TO *Robert Stewart*

DATE *Nov 4th*   TIME *9.40 a.m.*

CALLER

    NAME *Joanne Russett*

    NUMBER *0273 629104*   EXTENSION *337*

    ADDRESS ——

MESSAGE

The Health Awareness Seminar has been changed to Monday January 7th. Please ring and confirm that you still want to attend.

OPERATOR *Mary Thorp*

Formal messages should be:

    brief

    exact

    accurate

You should include the date the message was written or the date and time the telephone call was received.

Memorandums

A memorandum or memo is a handwritten or typewritten message which is used within an organization to convey information. It is usually written on pre-printed stationery by one individual to another, or it may be intended for a group of people. A memo provides a written record of a firm's business and is usually retained and filed.

Memos should be:

    written in sentences

    formal

    clear

    concise

11

T E S SERVICES

Financial Division

MEMORANDUM

FROM R Henry, Finance Manager   TO D Potts,
                                              Training Officer

REF   RH/MC/R/30/012   COPIES TO Mark Wilkins
DATE November 29th 1992   Wil Davies
                                                    Moira Larkin

SUBJECT   DISCIPLINARY PROCEDURE WORKSHOP,

December 3rd–5th 1992

Unfortunately Wil Davies is unable to attend the above course. I have agreed with Mark Wilkins that Moira Larkin should attend in his place.

I would be grateful if you could include Wil Davies on the next available course.

R Henry
Finance Manager

As memos are brief, it is important to consider the tone of your writing which should never be rude even if you are making a complaint or issuing a warning.

WRIGHTON COMMUNICATIONS plc

MEMORANDUM

TO All staff   SUBJECT Staff absence

FROM Anne Thomas   DATE September 14th 1992
     Personnel Officer

Although staff have been reminded of the procedures in two previous memos this year, difficulties are still arising because staff are failing to follow these instructions.

Procedure

1 Staff should telephone the departmental secretary on the first day of any illness, explaining the nature of the illness.

2 On returning to work, all staff should complete company sickness record form D273.

3 Anyone absent for reasons of illness for more than three days needs to complete a self-certification form which is available from health centres.

4 If you are absent for reasons of illness in excess of seven days, we require a certificate from your doctor.

** Write a memo using the standard memo format for the situation given below.

You need to send a memo to the maintenance department within your organization to complain about its failure to carry out certain work after your section moved to a new office on Thursday morning. Word processors have not been wired to the laser printer; a metal book shelf hasn't been built properly; the fire door sticks and the bottom drawer of the filing cabinet, which holds standard forms, was damaged in the move and now doesn't open. Your memo should be brief, exact, clear and contain only relevant information.

Notices

Notices are often used at work to pass on information which will be of interest and concern to a large number of employees. If you are writing a notice, you should consider wording and layout.

You want your notice to attract attention and be read. It should be:

brief but meaningful;

easily understood;

clearly laid out;

polite;

relevant.

CAR MILEAGE

All car mileage claims for November should be completed and sent to Victoria Milward by December 2nd. Claims received after this date cannot be included in employees' December pay cheques.

PETER FAIRLEY
EXPORT MANAGER

** Design a clear notice for the following situation.

Your firm has acquired a minibus which will be used to take clients to sites, presentations, meetings, etc. If staff want to use the minibus, they will need to show you their driving licences so that you can check them and note down the details. It is also a good idea for staff to have a practice drive before they take clients out. You will keep a booking diary and the booking forms will be in your office. It is obviously sensible for staff to make bookings as far in advance as possible as the minibus will probably be very popular. There will be a log sheet inside the minibus which staff must fill in each time they use it. There are 15 passenger seats and there is room for 2 wheelchairs to be clamped in the centre aisle. The minibus also has a wheelchair lift.

Instructions

If you are asked to write instructions for other colleagues, take care to consider your audience. Instructions need to be:

as brief as possible;

arranged in a logical order (usually in numbered points).

Use words that you know your audience will understand, clear headings and an uncluttered layout.

Compare the following two sets of instructions for their effectiveness in terms of style, vocabulary and layout.

A

Guidelines for Interviewers

Date and time

1 Give careful consideration to the date and time of each interview. You will need to allow adequate time so that you do not rush the interviewee. It is also important that you do not keep interviewees waiting.

Planning

2 Consider the purpose of the interview and what you want to achieve.

3 Study all the available information about the candidate.

4 Decide upon the areas you must cover.

5 Prepare questions that will elicit information from the candidate which is appropriate to the job for which you are interviewing.

B

Guidelines for Interviewers

1 Think carefully about where and when. Give yourself lots of time as there's nothing worse than hurrying some poor, nervous candidate. Don't let the person spend a long time waiting around for you to start while you finish your coffee.

2 Think about why you are interviewing the person and what you hope to get from it.

3 Have a good look through all the stuff you've got on the candidate.

4 Make up your mind about the things you want to get done in your interview.

5 Don't leave it until the day. The night before, think about the questions you're going to ask as you want to get as much out of the candidate as you can.

11

A has	B uses
formal vocabulary, tone and style;	chatty vocabulary;
	an informal tone;
a brief, exact and clear style;	a wordy and vague style;
a relevant tone and clear headings.	irrelevant asides and no headings.

** Write a brief set of instructions to colleagues in your workplace. It can be about anything that is appropriate to your situation. Look back through this chapter and identify formal words and phrases to help you to write your instructions.

Job descriptions

These may be given to us when we apply for a job or when we start working for an organisation. The format varies according to the organisation but the content always includes details of the post holder's duties and responsibilities.

ASSESSMENT ASSISTANT

Job summary To deal with housing benefit claims for private tenants in accordance with the appropriate regulations and procedures.

Accountability The post holder is responsible to the Head of Section (Benefits) in the Housing Department.

Job content

Main duties include

1 assessing claims for housing benefit;

2 inputting information into the computer system;

3 determining eligibility for rent allowance;

4 dealing with overpayments of housing benefit;

5 interviewing members of the public to provide information about eligibility for claims;

6 responding to tenants' requests and concerns regarding their benefit claims;

7 undertaking appropriate clerical and administrative duties and any other duties as agreed with the Head of Section (Benefits).

Sometimes an employee is asked to write his or her own job description. Advice will normally be given about format and house style and it will be checked by your manager to ensure that it is correct, but it may still seem a daunting task.

Helpful Hints

▶ The language used in a job description is

formal

precise

impersonal

Compare these sentences.

<u>You'll</u> have to answer the '<u>phone</u>.

personal pronoun   contractions

informal style

The <u>post holder</u> <u>is responsible for</u> dealing with telephone calls.

third person   precise wording

formal style

Ideas can also be expressed in indirect language.

e.g. All equipment must <u>be checked</u> by the post holder before it is allocated.

passive verb

Compare:

The post holder must <u>check</u> all equipment before allocating it.

active verb

11

▶ In the example of the job description given on page 154 the job is described in a series of points. A job description can also be written as a piece of continuous text.

> The post holder is responsible for the assessment of claims for housing benefit and determining tenants' eligibility for rent allowance. This information must be entered into the computer system. Housing benefit overpayment claims are dealt with in accordance with the standard guidelines.
>
> The post holder provides advice on eligibility to the public, and responds to tenants' requests and concerns regarding their claims.
>
> Other duties, including clerical and administrative tasks, are carried out as determined by the Head of Section (Benefits).

** Rewrite this job description, which is given as a list of separate points, as a piece of continuous writing.

Evening Reception Worker

Job summary To staff the leisure centre and supervise the building, Monday–Friday between 6.00 pm and 10.00 pm.

Accountability The post holder is responsible to the Manager of the leisure centre.

Main duties are:

    1 staffing the reception area;

    2 receiving payments for use of the leisure centre;

    3 arranging bookings for the centre;

    4 supervising the building;

    5 dealing with telephone calls;

    6 ensuring availability of sauna, solarium and fitness room;

    7 providing equipment to centre users;

    8 ensuring the centre is secure and alarmed when leaving;

    9 other duties as requested by Manager.

Reports

While you may not be required to write a formal report (see page 160) when you are at work, there will probably be occasions when you have to provide a short report on:

a product

a service

a piece of equipment

an incident

an event

a person

The report will be concerned with a factual situation but it may contain your own opinions or those of other people. It is usually written for a specific audience.

e.g. Your manager is thinking of buying a new photocopier. He might ask you to find out what type would be most suitable for your office, to compare various models and to decide which would be most suitable.

The tone and style of language used in a report is very similar to that used in a job description.

Use a   formal

precise

concise   approach

impersonal

Helpful Hints

▶ Gather your information in note form and plan your report carefully. You will need to write a draft copy and proof-read it carefully.

▶ Include only relevant facts or opinions.

▶ Give accurate details or assessments.

▶ Organise the information in a logical order, using main and sub headings. It may be helpful to the reader if you number the points you make.

▶ Give your report an appropriate heading. Reports are usually dated and signed at the end.

▶ You will probably need to summarise the information you wish to include in the report – keep the report as brief as possible. (Chapter 8 gives help with summary skills.)

▶ Consider how much your audience already knows about the subject. Avoid using technical language unless you know your reader will understand it.

EXAMPLE:

You recently attended a training seminar on word processing and your line manager has asked you to produce a report.

<u>Training seminar on Wordperfect,</u>
<u>attended 23 November 1992</u>

This session introduced participants to Wordperfect and provided practice in some of its basic functions.

<u>Content</u>

1 Explanation of the status line (the information displayed at the bottom of the screen).

2 Saving a document.

3 Closing down a machine.

4 Printing.

5 Emboldening and underlining.

6 Changing margins and setting tabs.

7 Mail merge.

<u>Methods</u>

The trainer demonstrated the function keys. Participants then worked through practice texts, following the instructions in the training package.

<u>Comments</u>

1 This session provided beginners with a useful introduction to Wordperfect. Experienced members of staff might prefer a more rapid delivery.

2 Wordperfect appears to be a suitable wordprocessing programme for our department. It is easy to use and its training package contains clear instructions.

<u>Recommendations</u>

1 A key member of staff should attend the next series of Wordperfect training sessions.

2 It should then be decided whether Wordperfect becomes the preferred word processing programme for this section.

** Use these notes to write a brief report in which you outline the main features of each photocopier described below and make a recommendation about which should be bought.

Proposed Purchase of Photocopier

Possible models

Tonsan TS 1000: price £800, desktop.
Features: enlargement/reduction of original; can copy in five colours: black, red, blue, green, purple; A4 and A5 paper sizes; produces up to 99 copies in one print run; 8 copies produced per minute.

Reno 542X: price £1000, desktop – but can buy optional work station.
Features: enlargement/reduction of original – pre-set or adjustable control; variety of editing functions; 30 copies per minute; A3, B4, A4, A5 and foolscap paper sizes. Optional extras: automatic document feed, sorter, editing system.

Formal reports

As you have seen, all reports are formal documents. You may be required to write formal reports which follow your company's house style and have to be organised under agreed headings. The following headings are sometimes used in formal reports.

Terms of Reference (This tells the reader who asked for the report and what the purpose of the report is.)

Procedure (This outlines the methods used to obtain the information.)

Findings (The main content of the report is presented under this heading.)

Conclusions (This is where the writer sums up the information.)

Recommendations (The writer will make suggestions based on the contents and conclusions of the report.)

Standard replies and circular letters

Standard replies are sent out in response to queries or requests when a general, non-specific reply is adequate. They may also be sent to acknowledge a complaint while it is being investigated, or to notify a customer of the despatch of an order.

EXAMPLE:

Ferndown Horticulture
45–49 Southampton Road
Ferndown
Dorset

Date as postmark

Dear Customer,

Thank you for the interest you have shown in our products. We are sending you a copy of our brochure, together with a current price list, and look forward to receiving your order in due course.

Please contact us if you require any further information.

Yours sincerely,

R Patel

Mrs R. Patel
Customer Services Manager

Note that:

▸ The letter has a formal style.

▸ The writer uses the pronoun 'we' when referring to the company.

▸ As this is a standard letter the recipient's address is not included nor is the letter dated.

▸ The tone of this letter is efficient yet friendly. The tone of standard letters must be appropriate for the purpose even though they are sent to a number of people.

EXAMPLE:

> The Wild West Theme Park
> Thorne Park
> Richmond
> Yorkshire
> KN4 6HZ
> Tel (0342) 6543333
> Fax (0342) 654334
>
> Dear Visitor
>
> Welcome to the Travel Show and thank you for visiting our stand.
>
> As you will see from our brochure, we offer what we consider to be the best value-for-money deal of any comparable entertainment park in Britain.
>
> You can enjoy an entire day of excitement, rides and attractions for only £5.00 per person. During that day you will also be able to watch action-packed live entertainment and take part in family fun events.
>
> When you've read through our brochure we're sure you'll agree that for a real family day out at a price you can afford, it has to be The Wild West Theme Park.
>
> See you soon!
>
> Yours sincerely,
>
> *Sian Dixon*
>
> Sian Dixon
> Park Manager

Note that:

▸ The language and tone are informal.
▸ When sending circular letters out by post, some companies personalise the greeting. The letters are identical but the company will use a mailing list of names and so is able to address each recipient personally.

Agendas and minutes

Agendas

These are sent to participants before a meeting to inform them of:

  the date, time, place of meeting;

  the points that will be considered at the meeting.

EXAMPLE:

You are invited to attend a meeting of the Canteen Management Group on Thursday 12 November 1992 at 3.30 pm.

AGENDA

1 To receive apologies for absence and welcome visitors

2 To confirm the minutes of the meeting on 4 September 1992

3 To deal with matters arising from the minutes

4 To consider complaints about seating arrangements

5 To discuss a continuation of the smoking ban

6 To receive a financial report

7 Any other business

8 Date of next meeting

Copies to:

  Mr Carter (chairman)
  Miss Allworthy
  Mr Bodington
  Mrs Lei
  Mr Poynton
  Miss Singleton

As participants will not want to read a wordy document, an agenda should be as brief as possible with a clear layout so that readers can immediately identify the proposed content of the meeting.

Minutes

These are the formal record of a meeting.

EXAMPLE:

MINUTES OF THE CANTEEN MANAGEMENT GROUP
meeting held on November 12 1992

Present: Mr Carter (chairman), Miss Allworthy, Mrs Lei, Mr Poynton, Miss Singleton

1 Apologies for absence were received from Mr Bodington. The chairman welcomed Mr Turner from Accounts.

2 The minutes of the previous meeting held on 4 March were confirmed as a true record.

3 There were no matters arising.

4 The chairman outlined the present seating arrangements in the canteen. Mrs Lei explained that several members of staff had complained about the division of the seating area into management and staff areas. Mr Poynton agreed that canteen staff were not satisfied with these arrangements as difficulties arose during busy times. It was agreed that a working party should be set up to investigate the views of all employees.

Section 2

Minutes of meetings are:

concise accounts of the relevant details;

written in formal language;

arranged under numbered points that correspond to the item numbers on the agenda;

written in indirect speech, using the past tense.

11

direct speech: "Canteen staff are not satisfied," stated Mr Poynton.

actual words spoken

indirect speech: Mr Poynton stated that canteen staff were not satisfied.

163

Final thoughts

While the writing tasks that you have been shown in this chapter are set in work situations, there may be occasions when you will need to tackle the same types of writing task as part of your social or leisure activities. For example, as a secretary of your local sports club you might be asked to write a report on the facilities offered at the club house.

The formal writing activities in this chapter demand a precise, formal tone, style and vocabulary. With practice, you will become accustomed to the vocabulary and phrases that make up a large part of business writing. The construction of precise, concise sentences and paragraphs will soon require less conscious effort and become a natural part of your writing style.

12
Essays

An essay is a piece of continuous writing; it can be a few hundred words or several thousand. You may be asked to write an essay:

as part of your coursework;

for homework;

as part of a project;

in an examination;

to read to others in your study group as a basis for discussion.

An essay is one way of assessing our knowledge about a subject and it is **a supreme test of our formal writing skills**.

What are the skills needed in formal writing?

Section 2

12

We have already dealt with many of these skills in previous chapters. In this chapter we will concentrate on applying these skills to essay writing.

Understanding and answering the question

Before you begin to gather ideas and make a plan, read the question carefully.

Ask yourself

| What does the question mean? Try expressing the question in your own words. | What do I need to include in my answer? | What type of essay is it? Must I relate facts, give examples, argue, analyse, describe... ? | How long should my essay be? |

At all stages of the essay-writing process: gathering ideas, planning, writing, proof-reading, ask yourself:

▶ Am I answering the question?
▶ Are the points relevant?
▶ Have I included all the main points?
▶ Have I given enough examples to illustrate my main points?
▶ Have I described, analysed, persuaded or narrated as the question asked?

It is worth spending some time analysing the question as it is all too easy to write the essay you would like to write instead of the one you have been asked to write. In exams, when you are feeling pressurised, it is particularly easy to misread a question. There will be more advice on exam practice later in the chapter.

Content

Select your material carefully. The great temptation is to write all you know about a subject instead of selecting the most appropriate or interesting content. Be ruthless in the planning stage and disregard:

ideas which have little evidence to support them;

details which detract from the main point;

points which are only peripheral to the subject.

When you have chosen the appropriate content, write with confidence and enthusiasm.

Gathering ideas and planning

In Chapter 7 you looked at a variety of ways of organising your ideas into an effective essay plan. You might like to go back to Chapter 7 to remind yourself of the main points. It is vital to organise your ideas if you are to produce a well-structured, coherent and fluent essay.

When you are studying you will be expected to consult several sources before you write an essay. You may even be expected to provide evidence of your reading by including quotations or a bibliography (a list, at the end of your essay, of all the books you have consulted). Chapter 8 gives you advice on summarising and note taking which will help you in your research.

CARRYING OUT RESEARCH FOR AN ESSAY

Select the relevant sources.

Make careful notes from each source

Collect together your notes from each source and, after carefully considering the question, plan your essay.

REMEMBER

Copy down quotations accurately and use quotation marks. Don't forget to mention the author and source.

Express your information in your own words. Your essay shouldn't be a collection of extracts from a variety of books.

Express facts accurately.

Don't try to pass off your own opinions as facts.

Accurately record the details of books in your bibliography, including title, author and publisher.

When you have assembled all the necessary information, plan your essay. You will need to consider

the beginning,   the development,   the end.

The beginnings of the essay

First impressions are important. You need to attract and hold the reader's interest so that he or she will want to continue reading. The first paragraph sets the tone of the essay. Don't begin in a predictable way, e.g. 'The fog swirled all around me' as the first sentence of an essay entitled, 'Lost in the Fog'; or an obvious statement such as, 'At times we all wonder what life is about'.

▶ Create interest, atmosphere or surprise.

▶ You could begin with

    a question,

    a quotation,

    a relevant fact,

    a definition,

    a provocative statement, or

    an interesting opinion.

▶ Get to grips with the title immediately – don't write an irrelevant preamble.

** Consider each of these sentences as a beginning of an essay entitled, 'A Woman's Place is in the Home'.

1 A family is a good organisation.

2 Every woman should have the freedom of choice as to whether she stays at home or chooses to work.

3 This is an outmoded and patronising view of women.

4 I agree – a woman's place is in the home.

5 Recent advances in equality for women have not managed to eradicate this deplorable view of a woman's role.

** Write an interesting first sentence for each of the following essay titles.

1 Describe a contemporary figure whom you admire and account for your admiration.

2 Loneliness

3 'Joy riding' – how can the problem be solved?

4 My Earliest Memories

5 Journalists

6 The Good Old Days

When you have completed your opening sentences, you may like to discuss them with other people. Are they effective introductions?

The development of the essay

This is the 'meat' of your essay. Here you will develop each idea in turn, providing supporting evidence for each. Ideas should be logically arranged and one idea should flow fluently into the next. The reader shouldn't feel he is being presented with a series of individual ideas. It should seem as if each point has been carefully chosen to support and reinforce the one preceding it to form part of a coherent whole.

The end of the essay

Although the composition of the final paragraph depends on the type of essay you are writing, always plan your ending before you start writing. Some writers hope a suitable ending will occur to them as they write, or that the essay will end naturally when they have included all their information or ideas. However, it is possible to 'signal' the end of an essay in the final paragraph so that the reader feels satisfied by the ending.

Advice on endings

- Don't use hackneyed phrases to begin your final paragraph (e.g. 'to sum up', 'at the end', 'finally', 'in conclusion', etc.).
- Don't summarise everything you have said before.
- End strongly. Include an interesting opinion, recommendations or a provocative statement.
- You want your reader to feel stimulated and thoughtful so try to end positively.

** Consider how a reader might view each of these endings.

1 We queued longer than it took for the ride. ('A Day to Remember')

2 Mothers and housewives who are happy in that role have my greatest respect. ('A Woman's Place Is in the Home')

3 We must respect a woman's decision to make her own choice and not impose stereotypes upon women. ('A Woman's Place Is in the Home')

4 How are we to know whom we can trust? ('Journalists')

5 I believe the Greece of the twentieth century has just as much to offer me as the Greece I have read about in history books. ('Describe a country you would like to visit and explain why')

6 People enjoy satellite television. ('Satellite Television')

Sentences and paragraphs

Throughout this book we have stressed the importance of writing in sentences – **sentences are the basis of all writing**. When you are engrossed in a subject or writing at length, it is sometimes easy to forget about writing in sentences. Candidates in examinations can worry so much about the content of their essays that they pour out their ideas without attending to sentence structure.

▶ As each sentence is a unit of sense, never begin to write a sentence until you have considered how you will complete it. Clumsy, ambiguous sentences can result if you ignore this advice.

▶ Use a variety of sentence lengths and structures.

▶ Each sentence should be a clear, straightforward expression of an idea, fact or opinion.

▶ When you proof-read your writing, be prepared to rewrite sentences which don't sound right or exactly express what you feel or want to say.

** Rewrite each of these ambiguous sentences so that the meaning will be clear to the reader.

1 There will be a meeting on bicycles in Conference Room B.

2 The local education committee has requested a report on children's diets to find out if they are unbalanced.

3 Karl Rawson saw the girl jumping through a knot-hole in the fence.

4 You will not catch cold germs walking in the fresh air.

5 Our spaniel eats anything and likes children.

6 We now have ninety pairs of red wellingtons on our hands.

7 Baskets of every shape and size hang from the oak beams woven in intricate designs.

8 The bishop walked among the guests eating their caviar.

When you plan your essay, you should find that an idea and its supporting evidence will form a paragraph. Essays must be written in paragraphs – failure to do so can lead to rambling, unstructured essays which could confuse the reader.

- Concentrate on a key sentence in each paragraph.
- Avoid too many short paragraphs.
- Avoid very long paragraphs. Can they be broken into smaller units of sense?
- Find a way of linking paragraphs together to produce a fluent piece of writing.

Spelling, punctuation and grammar

Your grasp of the conventions of standard English affects all areas of your writing, not only English essays.

Spelling

- Poor spelling lets you down and in some exams you will lose marks for it. Use techniques and learn rules which will help you to improve your spelling.

- Be careful not to misspell a word that is used in the title, a 'technical' word which is common in your subject area, or a word that you have encountered in your research. Copy words correctly.

- Use a dictionary to check any spellings you are uncertain of. Don't check each 'suspect' word as you write it or this will interrupt the flow of your writing and undermine your confidence in your ability to write and spell. Underline words and check them when you have completed your essay.

Punctuation

- Use sufficient punctuation to make your meaning clear. Remember the addition or omission of a comma can cause confusion.

  e.g. However, many candles we light at St Martin's we shall not be able to take away the shadows. ✗

  However many candles we light at St Martin's, we shall not be able to take away the shadows. ✓

- Use question marks where necessary, but avoid asking too many direct questions. As a device to retain the reader's interest, it can become tedious.

- Dialogue must be in quotation marks. Avoid using too much dialogue as it can be tiresome for the reader and tedious for you to punctuate. Any dialogue should be brief, interesting and serve a useful purpose.

Grammar

There is often a difference between the structures we use for speech and those used in writing. Characters, expressing themselves in passages of dialogue, don't have to be grammatically correct; indeed, ungrammatical conversation is often appropriate for the character. However, the rest of our writing must be grammatically correct so that we can impart our message clearly.

Vocabulary

A good vocabulary allows you to write freely, expressing yourself accurately and vividly. It adds interest and colour to your writing, and allows you to adopt an appropriate tone or degree of formality.

▶ Avoid repetition in your essays – use a thesaurus to find an alternative word. A few carefully chosen words can replace long phrases, making your writing more concise.

▶ Don't use long words to impress.

▶ If you are uncertain about the meaning of a word, check it in your dictionary.

▶ Avoid abbreviations, e.g. 'mins' for 'minutes', 'don't' for 'do not'. Conversational contractions are only permissible when used in dialogue.

A formal style and tone

The way we compose our sentences, the use of correct grammatical constructions, and appropriate vocabulary allows us to write in a formal style and convey a formal tone. In formal writing, avoid:

colloquial words or expressions

slang

jargon

tautology

vague words or phrases

everyday similes, e.g. 'as white as a sheet', 'as black as thunder'. Create your own vivid comparisons.

Proof-reading

Proof-reading is essential. We all make mistakes as we write, when our brains produce ideas more quickly than we can write them down.

Have you answered
the question?

Have you written in sentences?
Are there any long, unwieldy or
ambiguous sentences?

Are your sentences grouped
into logical paragraphs?

```
                    ⎛    The     ⎞
grammar ─────────── ⎜ proof-reading ⎟ ─────── spelling
                    ⎝   check    ⎠
```

grammar ─────────── The proof-reading check ─────── spelling

vocabulary   punctuation

Have you used words in their correct contexts?
Could you use a more interesting or precise word?
Is your language appropriate for your audience?

** Read the essay overleaf which describes a jumble sale. Consider each of the
essay-writing skills in turn and assess the writer's skills. When you have
formed your own opinions about the essay, compare them with the
suggestions in the **Answers**.

12

The Jumble Sale

The sale was due to start at 3 p.m. a large crowd had congregated at the front of the ramshackle village hall. Many had queued for a considerable time in the biting November wind in order to be among the first through the doors to secure the best bargains.

Elderly ladies waited anxiously to find a warm coat to keep out the cold, or woolen garments which they could unpick during the long winter evenings then knit into gloves and scarfs for their grandchildren. The affluent ladies of Emphington intended to scour the stalls for suitable materials to convert into patchwork quilts or cushions. For the poorer inhabitants jumble sales provided the opportunity to clothe both themselves and their children.

As the door swung slowly open, the orderly file of women charged forward as if about to commence a full-scale battle. All conversation ceased – the 'enemy' had been engaged.

Formal, neat piles of sorted garments were ransacked by the pushing hordes. Clothes were selected, scrutinised and secured into plastic carriers while others were rejected and tossed aside, only to be seized triumphantly by another bargain hunter. Battle was intense but brief.

Within half an hour the experienced customers sat in sagging, striped canvas chairs, their purchases hugging at their feet. Drinking weak tea out of cracked cups. Aloofly they surveyed the carnage they had created which was now being delicately picked over by the more inexperienced villagers.

By 4.15 the caretaker and his two assistants warily entered the hall to attempt to fold up the trestle tables and canvass chairs. They stuffed the remnants of the sale into large black dustbin liners to store it away for future occasions. Silence reigned in the dusty hall. The jumble sale army had retreated into their cottages to peruse their purchases and recount their tales of conquest.

Preparing to write

If you are to write effective and interesting essays, it helps to be able to draw upon a good store of background knowledge.

Wide reading is essential. It gives you facts and opinions on which you can base your own judgements. Read as many different sources as possible, both non-fiction and fiction, from books, newspapers and magazines.

Television and radio are valuable sources for information and ideas.

Listen to other people's views and experiences and try to discuss ideas with them. In a good discussion you will need to present your views as persuasively as possible and back them up with evidence. This will be good practice and will help you tackle discursive essays.

You may like to keep a **diary of your personal experiences and observations.** Many authors note down interesting events, descriptions of places, details of people they have met or snatches of conversation so that they can develop them later in their writing.

Whenever you have any spare time, **practise.** Instead of repeatedly glancing at your watch as you wait for a train to depart, write a descriptive paragraph about the platform outside your carriage or the occupants within it.

Types of essays

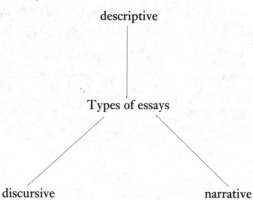

Although the advice given here is directly relevant to English essays, it can also apply to essays in other subjects, particularly the guidance about discursive essays.

Many essays cannot be categorised as one type. For example, an account of the evacuation of a village requires both descriptive and narrative skills.

Descriptive essays

You may be asked to describe a person, place, event, experience or process. Whatever you describe, your description should be crisp, interesting and vivid. It will be awarded higher marks if it accurately captures the essence of the subject.

People

Don't concentrate on their physical appearances: include details about their mannerisms, behaviour, tones of voice and ways of speaking, interests, fears, personalities and reactions to others.

Your description should be convincing and realistic. It is usually easier to base your description wholly or partially on someone you know.

You may decide to describe a person's character from his or her actions and behaviour as Margaret Forster has in this extract from *The Seduction of Mrs Pendlebury*.

It was a long time before Alice went inside. Her daughter slept, her husband was not yet home, and if the truth were told she was a little depressed by inside. She had no confidence in it, failing to recognize the ugly pieces of furniture that seemed to fit nowhere. Passing them, all heaped together till she decided where they should go, she was given to kicks and curses. Most of the stuff had been her mother's. Why, when she had had her pick, why she had chosen such horrid pieces she did not know. Laura, her sister, had gone with her to the house and told her to pick first, anything, everything she wanted and she had made all the wrong choices which she must now put up with, not having the skill to disguise her lack of taste.

There was, however, supper to make. She had to watch her dreamy state. Trying to overcome the dangerous apathy that could at times engulf her, she had trained herself to observe certain rituals that Tony and Amy might not suffer. Neither would complan if there was no supper but her own remorse would hurt her. So she chopped vegetables, liking the textures and colours, and trimmed meat and laid the table, an island of bare board among crowded surfaces. She liked doing it, it gave her an easiness she was always looking for. Without such tasks she was a mess, having nothing she wanted to do and watching always for the slide into listlessness. Everything was ready when Amy woke and Tony came home.

They were a silent, non-talking couple, alarming to be with, so little was said. Sometimes they talked in a stilted way as though talking was something that must be done or the art would be lost.

12

By choosing appropriate dialogue for your person, you can also bring out facets of their character.

** Look at this short description of Monsieur Fructus in which we learn about the man's looks, taste in clothes, driving style, way of walking, accent and manner.

> It was early evening when the car pulled up in a cloud of dust. The driver had obviously come to the wrong house. He was young and dark and good-looking, resplendent in the costume of a 1950s saxophone player – a wide-shouldered drape jacket shot through with gleaming threads, a lime-green shirt, capacious trousers that narrowed to hug his ankles, shoes of dark blue suede with bulbous crêpe soles, a flash of turquoise socks.
>
> 'Fructus, Thierry. *Agent d'assurance.*' He walked into the house with short, jaunty steps. I half expected him to start snapping his fingers and make a few mean moves across the floor. I offered him a beer while I got over my surprise, and he sat down and gave me the benefit of his vibrant socks.
>
> '*Une belle mesong.*' He had a strong Provençal accent which contrasted strangely with the clothes, and which I found reassuring. He was businesslike and serious, and asked if we were living in the house all year round; the high rate of burglaries in the Vaucluse, he said, was partly due to the large number of holiday homes. When houses are left empty for ten months a year, well ... the shoulders of his jacket escalated in an upholstered shrug.
>
> (from *A Year In Provence* by Peter Mayle)

Write a short description of someone you know. Include some of the descriptive elements that Peter Mayle uses in his description of Monsieur Fructus.

Places, events and experiences

▶ Many writers describe what they see, neglecting the other senses: smell, hearing, taste and touch. To give your descriptions colour and originality, try to include a variety of senses.

▶ It isn't necessary or desirable to include everything in a description; concentrate on the most interesting or unusual features. Details about a particular aspect can bring your reader from the general 'view' to the specific. For example, if you were writing about a deserted cottage, you could begin by describing its overall appearance and then describe in detail one downstairs window that caught your attention and imagination.

▶ Create atmosphere by choosing appropriate vocabulary. If you want to paint a picture of tranquillity, it is not enough to mention 'a tranquil scene'. You should describe particular aspects which contribute to the sense of tranquillity and could use words such as hush, peace, stillness, serenity, repose, placid, untroubled and undisturbed.

▶ It often helps to provide atmosphere by creating a contrast. If you want to portray the frenetic bustle of a busy mainline railway station, you may, having described it, compare it to your friend's country cottage at the end of your journey – a haven of peace and solitude. Contrasting vocabulary will help your reader to envisage the noisy activity of the station more accurately.

Busy station	Quiet cottage
congested, crushed, huddled,	deserted, undisturbed, silent,
swarming, teeming, thronged,	secluded, privacy, isolation,
overflowing, clamour,	noiseless, soundless
commotion, hubbub	

Processes

A description of, for example, a technical process need not be a collection of accurately related chronological happenings. An essay such as this benefits from the use of descriptive vocabulary and phrases which allow you not only to describe the process concisely and accurately but also to attract the attention and interest of your reader.

If you were asked to write an essay entitled 'How Women Gained the Vote', you would need to present accurate facts in a chronological order. A short, vivid account of women chained to railings or a description taken from a newspaper report of the day would add detail and support the facts. The more descriptively you write, the more meaningful and memorable the scene is for your audience.

Narrative essays

In a narrative essay you may write an account based on factual information, real-life experience or you may invent a story. You might be asked to write a story where you are given the first or last sentence. Some people are talented at inventing original stories: others are better narrating a personal experience or devising a story which is partially based on experience.

▶ Don't waste time with a long preamble to set the scene – gain your reader's attention in as lively a manner as possible.

▶ The story should be realistic and interesting, but if you include too many events you will only be able to mention each briefly. It is better to adopt a simple story with the minimum number of events taking place over a short period of time. Include plenty of description to create atmosphere and involve your reader.

▶ Events should be arranged in a logical sequence. You may, however, decide to adopt the 'flashback' approach where you begin with an event at or near the end of your story and then recount the sequences leading up to this final event.

▶ The story should have a well-planned, plausible ending. Too many stories peter out with the character waking up from a dream or fading into unconsciousness.

▶ Describe the feelings of the participants or use dialogue to allow them to express their own views.

Discursive essays

In discursive essays you examine a subject, consider facts and opinions, weigh up arguments and, sometimes, structure them into a personal recommendation or conclusion. This is perhaps the most difficult type of essay to write as it requires careful analytical and organizational skills.

You could be asked to write a discursive essay for any subject you are studying.

EXAMPLES:

English – Video 'nasties' are sometimes cited as one of the main causes of our increasingly violent society. To what extent is this true?

History – Assess the achievements of Mussolini's foreign policy.

Management Studies – Describe your office structure and examine and account for its strengths and weaknesses.

Such essay titles will use words like 'assess', 'account for', 'examine', 'discuss', 'comment on', 'what were the causes', 'explain', 'do you agree', 'what effects', 'consider', etc.

According to the wording of the question, you will need to:

> weigh up the pros and cons of the subject,

> look only at either the pros or cons,

> use facts and/or opinions to build up your assessment of a subject or situation.

Helpful Hints

▶ Determine what the question requires of you.

▶ Think about your own viewpoint, making certain you have adequate evidence to support it. Don't change your opinion half way through your essay. Writers of discursive essays often make the mistake of describing events, processes, facts, etc. without commenting on them – they are not answering the question.

▶ Present your ideas clearly and logically, and, if necessary, persuasively.

▶ Consider the arguments or opinions of others too. You might choose to outline your arguments first, and then present the arguments of the other side before establishing your conclusion. Alternatively, you may find you are more successful at putting the counter-arguments first, followed by a strong expression of your own arguments which will then lead you directly into your conclusion. When you practise writing this type of essay, it is useful to try both routes to establish which produces the more effective essay.

▶ Don't express yourself in vague, inaccurate generalisations such as 'Everyone over fifty is content to ...' or 'Many people think ...'.

▶ If you are writing a timed essay or are restricted to a word count, don't attempt to examine too many issues. You need a brief paragraph of introduction and a final strong paragraph. This only leaves you time and space to explore three or four issues.

Advice on writing essays

As you practise writing essays you will begin to **appreciate which type of essay you are best at**. In an exam or assessment situation, if there is a choice, choose the type of essay you can deal with most effectively.

Whichever essay you write, it is important to **decide on the tense**. It is usually easier to write in the past tense because the majority of events or experiences we describe or narrate have already occurred. Writing in the present tense can be particularly effective and vivid if you are writing a story as it allows your reader to feel he is part of the action. However, it can be difficult to sustain. The choice of tense is yours. The important thing is that you are consistent throughout an essay and do not keep changing tense.

Examination practice

Writing essays in exams is a daunting task for most of us as we feel nervous when writing 'against the clock'.

Study past exam papers in the subject so that you know:

what type of questions to expect,

the layout of the paper,

the instructions on the paper.

Practise completing individual questions and an entire paper under exam conditions. **Work out how much time you should spend on each question.** You will need to allow time to plan and check each answer. **Even in an exam situation, planning is essential.** Do not be panicked into feeling you have insufficient time to plan. If you have worked out the timing of questions at an early stage in your course, you will be used to dividing up your time.

For example, if you are answering a question in an hour, a sensible time allocation might be:

10–15 minutes for planning,

40–45 minutes for writing,

5–10 minutes for checking.

With practice you will discover the division of time that is right for you.

Read the paper very carefully. It is easy to misread questions when you are nervous. When you have a choice of questions, select wisely. Try to choose questions which:

you are confident you can write about;

interest you;

are the types of essay you are good at.

Once you have started your essay, you won't have time to change your mind and start a different question.

Although you are writing quickly, your **handwriting must be legible**.

Confidence and practice

As you have worked through this book, you have been given opportunities to develop your writing skills in a variety of tasks and situations. The majority of people find it easier to express themselves in speech than in writing. We have all had the experience of knowing what we want to write but being unable to put it into writing. Believe in yourself – it happens to us all. If you are to become a more confident writer, you must practise writing regularly. As your writing improves you will gain more pleasure from writing which will make you want to write more. Follow the writing cycle.

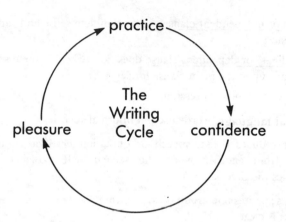

Understanding the Terms

adjective, describes or gives more information about a noun.

adverb, usually gives more information about a verb.

antonyms, words which have the opposite meaning to each other.

apostrophes, used for <u>contractions</u>, e.g. don't; *or* to show <u>ownership</u>, e.g. Mike's jumper.

clauses,

   <u>a main or independent clause</u> makes complete sense and can stand alone as a sentence;

   <u>subordinate or dependent clause</u> does not make complete sense by itself but depends upon the main clause for sense.

cliché, a stereotyped expression.

colloquial language, words used in informal speech.

colon, introduces a list, speech or quotation *or* divides one part of a sentence from another when the second half explains, expands or summarises the first half.

comma, separates one group of words from another so that the meaning of a sentence is clear.

conjunction, a word which links two parts of a sentence together.

consonant, any letter of the alphabet which is not a vowel.

dash, indicates a dramatic pause, an explanation or an interrupted conversation.

   <u>a pair of dashes</u>, separate asides, afterthoughts, opinions or non-essential information from the main thrust of the sentence.

essays,

   <u>descriptive essay</u>, an essay in which you describe a person, place, event, experience or process.

   <u>discursive essay</u>, an essay in which you examine a subject, considering facts, opinions, arguments and arrive at a conclusion.

narrative essay, an account based on facts, experience or an imagined story.

exclamation mark, used at the end of an exclamatory sentence and some commands.

full stop, used at the end of a sentence.

guidewords, words appearing in bold type at the top of a page in a dictionary or dictionary thesaurus which indicate the first and last complete entries on that page.

homophone, a word that sounds the same as another but has a different spelling and meaning.

jargon, the specialised language of a group of people who share a common interest, job, etc.

mnemonic, a memory device.

plural, more than one item.

prefix, a syllable or syllables added to the beginning of a word to alter the meaning of a word.

question mark, used at the end of a sentence where an answer is expected.

quotation marks, can be double ("") or single (' ') and are placed around the actual words a person says in a dialogue, or around a quotation.

semicolon, links two closely related sentences into one longer sentence. It can also be used to punctuate a long or complicated list.

sentences
  simple sentence, contains only one finite verb.

  double sentence, two simple sentences linked by a conjunction.

  multiple sentence, formed when three or more main clauses are linked by conjunctions.

  complex sentence, contains one or more main clauses and has at least one subordinate clause.

singular, one item.

subject of a sentence, who or what the sentence is about.

suffix, syllable or syllables added to the end of a word.

syllable, a word or part of a word which can be made by one effort of breath.

synonyms, words having the same or similar meanings.

tautology, an unnecessary repetition of the same idea in different words.

tense, the tense of a verb indicates the time when the action described takes place: present, past or future.

thesaurus, contains a collection of synonyms, related words and antonyms.

verb, expresses an action or indicates a state of being or having.

finite verb, a verb which has a subject.

vowels, the letters a, e, i, o and u.

Answers

NB No answers are given where you are asked to research words in a dictionary or thesaurus, where answers depend upon personal responses, or where a number of alternative answers is possible.

Chapter 2   Units of Sense – Sentences

Finite verb

1 is

2 was sent

3 will collect

4 welcomed

5 had been strewn

6 was

Complete sense

1 not a sentence

2 a sentence

3 not a sentence

4 not a sentence

5 not a sentence

6 not a sentence

7 not a sentence

8 a sentence

9 not a sentence

10 not a sentence

Suggested rewrite:

As soon as she entered the room, she knew a burglary had taken place. The window was open and a warm breeze filled the room. Piles of books and untidy heaps of clothes were everywhere. Drawers were half open. It was chaos.

Complex sentences

Suggestions:

1 The woman, with her blond hair carelessly arranged in a plait, entered the shop and joined the queue where she waited patiently to be served.

2 He adjusted his glasses and blew his nose vigorously while waiting for the previous speaker to finish.

3 The doctor, tired at the end of a long day, called his last patient into the consulting room.

4 When Tim had collected Angus, he drove them to Reeves Park where the town's first Rock Festival was being held.

5 He had to catch the coach from Alvechurch to Birmingham as the railway track was being electrified and no trains ran between 10 am and 5 pm.

6 Abdul lent his leather jacket to Andy as Andy had forgotten his keys and was unable to go home to change.

7 Alison spread out her papers, poured herself some water, fingered her necklace nervously, smoothed her skirt and took a deep breath before addressing the meeting.

8 Standing on the corner, he listened to the sound of the heavy artillery coming from the hills south of the town.

Chapter 3   Units of Sense – Paragraphs

Key sentences

Main ideas in the passage:

Paragraph 1: changes to the House of Commons during the recess.

Paragraph 2: stone plinths in the Members' Lobby.

Paragraph 3: the empty plinth.

Paragraph 4: the 'think metric' notice.

Paragraphing the passage:

The House of Commons changes during the recess. Like a stage when the curtains are drawn and the props dismantled, large parts of it simply disappear. Seemingly half the floorboards are raised, turning the corridors of power into hazardous catwalks, as scores of workmen lay wide, impressive-looking pipes. These are something to do with the new air-conditioning system. While the United States, which actually has hot weather, is learning to live without frozen air, the House of Commons, which is always in recess for two of the three summer months, is having it piped regardless of oil crises and Arabs. Huge quantities of furniture are moved from one place to another. Massive brown Chesterfields, displaced from the Smoking Room, line the Ways and Means corridor like slumbering hippos. Whole staircases are blocked off by multi-tiered piles of chairs. Vast rolls of carpet lie in wait to trip the hurrying visitor.

In the Members' Lobby, now sealed off from an inquisitive public by arches of polythene sheeting, they are working on two stone plinths which stand on either side of the exit towards the Central Lobby. On one, it is said, Clement Attlee will shortly be raised. He will join Churchill, Balfour, Joe Chamberlain and other petrified politicians gazing out on the scurrying and scheming which whirls around the lobby when the house is sitting.

The other plinth seems to be unaccounted for. One suggestion is that it should be devoted to the Unknown Lobby Correspondent. The sculptor would capture a facial expression devoted to world-weary cynicism and servility in equal measure, a pile of scruffy papers would be in his hand, and at his feet would stand the Eternal Gin and Tonic.

In the midst of the works, by the Commons rifle range, there was last week a large colourful notice headed THINK METRIC. Underneath was a drawing of a large foot, and the legend: "This is not a foot. It is 300 millimetres." Someone had scrawled underneath: "And who is going to 300 millimetre the bill for all this load of trash, then?"

(From *On the House* by Simon Hoggart)

Final thoughts

Main ideas:

<u>Paragraph 1</u>: a comparison of Japanese and British lunch boxes.

<u>Paragraph 2</u>: the Japanese attitude to food.

<u>Paragraph 3</u>: the Japanese diet and average cholesterol level.

<u>Paragraph 4</u>: benefits of the traditional Japanese diet.

Chapter 4   Punctuation in Practice

Testing out capital letters

Sarah Newton had intended to stay at the Hotel Imperial in Torquay for Christmas, but when she saw the advertisement in Pickfords Travel for winter holidays in Florida, she changed her mind. An American Christmas appealed to her so she rushed into the shop. "Have you any places left? I would like to go to Florida next Monday – that's Christmas Eve."

Lists

Claud was enthusiastic about his collection of toy soldiers, railway engines, stamps and carrier bags. He spent every Saturday morning dusting the soldiers, oiling the engines, and cataloguing the stamps and carrier bags. He would finger each new treasure slowly, deliberately and lovingly. His entire collection was housed in the enormous, mahogany wardrobe next to his bed.

Summing it up

1 However, I like Audrey.

2 Cliff entered the classroom with his wife, and his books in a carrier bag.

3 In particular, trousers are forbidden.

4 With this in mind, time will be available towards the end of the day.

Chapter 5   Spelling

Proof-reading

MEMORANDUM

To: All staff

From: <u>Personnel</u> Manager   **Date**: 8 September 1992

Subject: Thefts from cars

<u>There</u> have been <u>several</u> <u>instances</u> of thefts from cars parked in
Car Park A (Ewell Road) <u>recently</u>. The <u>security</u> officer has
<u>arranged</u> for <u>guards</u> to make <u>periodic</u> checks but your help is
also required. Please <u>ensure</u> your car is left locked and any
<u>valuable</u> articles are put out of <u>sight</u> in the boot. Report any
<u>suspicious</u> <u>incidents</u> to Mr Hallant (<u>chief</u> security officer).

Plurals

computers	alleys	boxes	pansies
tannoys	studios	stitches	wishes
churches	copies	proofs	suffixes

Possible and probable letter combinations

surgeon	thirst	circle
suffer	survive	earnest
furniture	purchase	early
suburb	merger	urgent

Chapter 6   Vocabulary

Referring to a thesaurus

Suggestions:

> The <u>dreary/murky</u> November day drew to a close. The grey
> mist which had <u>lingered</u> all day <u>prevented</u> the last weak traces
> of sunlight from <u>piercing</u> the gloom.
>   John walked along the streets, trampling through <u>mounds</u> of
> <u>sodden</u> leaves. His mood matched the <u>dismal/dreary/cheerless</u>
> weather – he was miserable, cold and <u>weary</u>. He thought of his
> home in Rarotonga: the <u>intense/fierce</u> heat of the sun, the

waves breaking on the coral reef and the <u>extensive</u> beaches of silver sand edged by <u>lofty, soaring</u> palm trees. It was an island paradise and he had <u>exchanged</u> it for a college course in Britain!

Guidelines

a wet night could be damp, humid, clammy, showery, gloomy, dull, sombre, cheerless, dismal or dreary.

a cherished pet might be glossy, well-fed, well-groomed, contented, satisfied, in good condition, spruce or well-nourished.

an effective speaker can be described as able, competent, effectual, compelling, convincing, forceful, impressive or persuasive.

an overgrown garden is chaotic, unkempt, uncontrolled or untidy.

Chapter 8   Summary Skills

'Champagne Flights'

<u>Main points</u>

flights all year

flight lasts one hour

receive a glass of champagne and a 'First Flight' certificate

returned to launch site

<u>Summary</u>

A flight in a hot air balloon takes one hour and is available throughout the year. At the end of your flight you will receive a glass of champagne, a 'First Flight' certificate and be taken back to the launch site.

Formal notes

No sub headings

No numbered points

No key words or phrases

Poor layout

Unclear meaning

<u>Suggestions for an article 'Accommodation for Walkers'</u>

If you are a member of the YHA you may like to use youth hostels. Details of the hostel locations are sent to you when you join. Charges are reasonable but you need to take your own sheet sleeping bag with you.

Walkers in the Peak District can find simple overnight shelter in camping barns. You need to take all your own equipment including that needed for sleeping and cooking.

If you have your own camping equipment you may decide to stay at official camping sites (details can be obtained from local tourist offices), or you could seek a landowner's permission to camp on his land.

Details of bed and breakfast accommodation can be obtained from local tourist offices. Although the charges are higher than at youth hostels, they represent good value for money.

Suggested notes:

How Women Can Protect Themselves

Sensible Precautions

1 At home

   a) **locks**

      i fit & use window locks

            door locks

            door chains

      ii get advice from police

               local DIY store

      iii change door locks when move to new house

   b) **telephone**

      i only give your number when answering

      ii in telephone directory, give only surname & initials

      iii obscene calls: replace receiver at once

                 make no response to caller

                 if persist, inform police/operator

                 record dates/times of calls

2 Walking

    i use well-lit main roads

    ii face on-coming traffic

    iii if followed, cross road

        hurry to other people

3 Motorist

  a) route

    i use main roads

    ii car: good order

       sufficient petrol

    iii leave details of route

    ETA

  b) parking

    i use well-lit streets/car parks

    ii on return – have keys ready

DON'T give lifts to hitch hikers

    stop to help unless genuine emergency

Chapter 9   Letters

Types of letters

1 semi-formal

2 formal

3 informal

4 semi-formal/informal

5 formal

6 formal

7 semi-formal

8 informal

First and last paragraphs

Suggested letter to Mr Collins:

Formal letter layout

Your name
Your address
The date

Mr Collins
Managing Director
Portman Engineering
Evensly Road
Luton

Dear Mr Collins

On Friday, 13 January, I tore my new leather jacket on the wire perimeter fence as I was leaving your company's car park.

The damage occurred as I was forced to squeeze between my car and the fence to avoid a deep pot-hole full of water. The car park is in a deplorable condition with numerous pot-holes, crumbling walls and broken fences. I understand that, despite a number of complaints from your employees, no action has been taken to make the car park safer to use.

I consider that it is the company's responsibility not only to pay for the repair to my jacket, but also to ensure the car park is maintained in a better condition so that similar incidents do not take place in the future. I would appreciate your comments on both points.

Yours sincerely.

Your signature
Print your name

Final thoughts

strengths	weaknesses
clear and correct layout	unclear and confusing message
formal tone	clumsy and contorted style (e.g. first paragraph)
correct spelling	incorrect closing phrase (should be Yours sincerely)
correctly divided into paragraphs	incorrect punctuation (note last paragraph)
	poor sentence structure throughout

Chapter 11   Business Writing

Memoranda

Suggested memo

MEMORANDUM

TO   name and position, maintenance department

FROM   your name and position

DATE   date you write memo

SUBJECT Maintenance Work

I would be grateful if you could complete the work which you have begun on my section's new office. The work still to be done includes:

1 Wiring the word processors to the laser printer.

2 Completing construction of a metal book shelf.

3 Ensuring the fire door opens freely.

4 Unjamming the bottom door of the filing cabinet (jammed in transit).

Items 1, 2 and 4 are causing inconvenience to my staff and affecting their efficiency. Item 3 is a potential safety hazard.

your signature

Notices

Suggestion:

NEW COMPANY MINIBUS

I am pleased to confirm that a minibus is now available for staff use.

The vehicle seats 15 passengers and has the facility for 2 people in wheelchairs to travel in the centre aisle – their wheelchairs can be clamped into position.

All staff wishing to use the minibus should present their driving licences to me for checking and it is advisable to have a practice drive before taking clients out.

Booking forms can be obtained from my office and I will keep the booking diary. Staff are advised to book well in advance.

It is important that staff complete the log sheet inside the minibus each time the vehicle is used.

your signature   date

Job descriptions

Suggestion:

Job description for an Evening Reception Worker

The post holder is responsible for staffing the reception area, receiving payments for the use of the leisure centre, arranging bookings and dealing with telephone calls. The building must be supervised during opening hours and secured with alarms when closed. It is necessary to ensure the availability of sauna, solarium, fitness rooms and that equipment is provided to centre users. The manager may require other duties to be undertaken.

Reports

Suggestion:

Proposed Purchase of Photocopier

Possible models

1 **Tonsan TS 1000** (price £800)

This desktop copier with an enlargement/reduction feature can copy in five colours – black, red, blue, green and purple. It will accept A4 or A5 paper and produces up to 99 copies in one print run, at the rate of 8 copies per minute.

2 **Reno 542X** (price £1000)

Although this is a desktop copier, an optional work station is available. It features a pre-set or adjustable control for enlargements and reductions and a variety of editing functions. Copies of either A3, B4, A4, A5 or foolscap size are produced at the rate of 30 per minute. The optional extras include an automatic document feed, sorter and editing system.

Recommendations

It is suggested that the **Reno 542X** be purchased. Although it is more expensive, it produces copies at a faster rate and is more flexible in terms of paper sizes. Our department does not require the colour facility of the Tonsan TS1000. If the Reno 542X were purchased, it would be possible to buy some or all of the optional extras later in order to maximise its potential.

Chapter 12 Essays

Beginnings

1 A vague way to begin an essay.

2 A clear and positive opening sentence.

3 Firm and positive.

4 Avoid such a beginning.

5 A firm and positive opening sentence.

Endings

1 This sentence doesn't sound like the ending to an essay.

2 A positive, personal ending.

3 The writer has completed the essay in a thoughtful way.

4 A question for the reader to contemplate.

5 The essay had been rounded off in a clear, firm manner.

6 An unconvincing ending.

Sentences and paragraphs
Suggestions:

1 There will be a meeting about bicycles in Conference Room B.

2 The local education committee has requested a report on whether children's diets are unbalanced.

3 Karl Rawson, looking through a knot-hole in the fence, saw the girl jumping.

4 You will not catch cold germs by walking in the fresh air.

5 Our spaniel eats anything and enjoys the company of children.

6 We now have ninety pairs of red wellingtons remaining.

7 Baskets of every shape and size, woven in intricate designs, hang from the oak beams.

8 The bishop walked among the guests as they ate their caviar.

Proof-reading the essay on a jumble sale

1 <u>Understanding and answering the question</u>
The title of the essay could be interpreted as narrative or descriptive – the author has chosen a descriptive answer.

2 <u>Content</u>
The material in the essay is relevant to the title.

3 <u>Planning</u>
The essay has obviously been planned as there is a logical order. The beginning is a little weak but the writer has tried to end on a strong note.

4 Sentences and paragraphs

The opening sentence should be divided into two: 'The sale was due to start at 3 p.m. A large crowd had congregated at the front of the ramshackle village hall.'

In the fifth paragraph, 'Drinking weak tea out of cracked cups' isn't a sentence: there is no subject.

The essay is logically divided into paragraphs which shows that time has been spent on planning.

5 Spelling, punctuation and grammar

In paragraph two the American version of the word 'woollen' has been used by mistake. In the last paragraph, 'canvas' (a type of durable cloth) has been misspelled as 'canvass' which means to solicit votes or opinions.

6 Vocabulary

Some interesting and appropriate language has been selected, with some vivid imagery and precise description used.

7 Style and tone

As the essay is grammatically correct and carefully constructed, a sense of formality is conveyed, even though the subject matter and content is quite light-hearted.

8 Proof-reading

Few errors – the essay has been proof-read.

Index